Kana de Manga

A fun, easy way to learn the ABCs of Japanese!

Text by Glenn Kardy Art by Chihiro Hattori

ひらがな (Hiragana)

あ a	い i	う u	え e	お o
か ka	き ki	く ku	け ke	こ ko
さ sa	し shi	す su	せ se	そ so
た ta	ち chi	つ tsu	て te	と to
な na	に ni	ぬ nu	ね ne	の no
は ha	ひ hi	ふ fu	へ he	ほ ho
ま ma	み mi	む mu	め me	も mo
や ya		ゆ yu		よ yo
ら ra	り ri	る ru	れ re	ろ ro
わ wa				を wo
				ん n

が ga	ぎ gi	ぐ gu	げ ge	ご go
ざ za	じ ji	ず zu	ぜ ze	ぞ zo
だ da	ぢ ji	づ zu	で de	ど do
ば ba	び bi	ぶ bu	べ be	ぼ bo
ぱ pa	ぴ pi	ぷ pu	ぺ pe	ぽ po

MANGA UNIVERSITY presents...

A fun, easy way to learn the ABCs of Japanese!

TOKYO SAN FRANCISCO

Manga University presents ... Kana de Manga
A Fun, Easy Way to Learn the ABCs of Japanese

Published by Japanime Co. Ltd.
2-8-102 Naka-cho
Kawaguchi-shi
Saitama 332-0022 Japan

Second edition
Printed in Japan in December 2004

Emily へ
Daddy から

CONTENTS

FOREWORD

Learning the Japanese phonetic alphabets of hiragana and katakana is perhaps the single most useful thing any visitor to Japan can do. The reason is that restaurant names, foreign terms and transportation signs use these visual alphabets. If you can pronounce the sound of these characters, you can get around easily and have more fun in Japan.

Hiragana (cursive form) and katakana (squared form) are the true "ABCs of Japanese," as they can be used to write words as well as complete sentences. Children in Japan learn to read and write hiragana and katakana (collectively known as kana) long before they are introduced to Chinese characters, or kanji. Also, most manga comic books targeted toward the youngest readers in Japan are written completely in kana.

Each kana page in this book has an easy-to-grasp manga cartoon image representing a sound that begins with the hiragana or katakana character featured prominently at the top of the page. A brief informative explanation accompanies each drawing; the English equivalent of the word is given; and there is a work area where the person studying can practice writing the kana forms.

This Manga University book has been prepared to make learning the phonetic sounds of Japanese kana systems both fun and effective. Educators know that language learning is enhanced through images and associations. This book builds on these principles by linking Japanese kana characters to Japanese images that anyone can readily identify.

So, don't waste any time! Make the investment. Once you master the kana characters in this book you will find a whole new world of Japan will be opened up to you.

Ronald A. Morse
Professor of Japan Studies, University of Nevada, Las Vegas

INTRODUCTION

Congratulations! When you purchased this book, you took a step into a whole new world – the world of reading and writing in Japanese. It's a world of endless possibility, and you'll find new doors opening as you learn each new character. Soon, you'll be able to read your favorite manga comics in their original language. You'll burst through the language barrier as you make Japanese friends online. And when you visit Japan, you'll be able to read signs, menus, maps and more on your own. There are hundreds of reasons to learn Japanese, and mastery of its most basic writing system is the best way to get started.

The two systems we'll be focusing on, hiragana and katakana, are phonetic syllabaries. Each one has 46 characters, called kana, which function much like English letters in that each has a specific pronunciation. Complete sentences can be written in kana by people who don't know kanji, the far more complex set of characters based on Chinese ideographs. Kana can be used to unlock these kanji characters, and are learned first by Japanese children and students of the language before they move on to kanji. By some estimates, there are more than 50,000 different kanji, but only about 2,000 are officially recognized by the Japanese Ministry of Education as frequently used characters. A fourth script, called romaji, is used to make Japanese readable to others by converting the characters into English, or "roman," letters. For instance, the title of this book, "Kana de Manga," is the romaji, or romanized, form of what would be written as かなでマンガ in Japanese.

USAGE AND PRONUNCIATION

In general, hiragana is used to write native Japanese words and inflections, while katakana is used to make foreign words readable to the Japanese.

Katakana is also often used for the names of plants and animals. In both hiragana and katakana, each character represents a syllable, as opposed to letters in the English language. There are more kana than letters, of course, but don't worry – they're quite easy to memorize. To help you get started, we've written each kana in romaji on the charts in the front and back of this book.

There are five basic vowel sounds in spoken Japanese:

a as in ***ah***
i as in s**ee**
u as in y***ou***
e as in n**e**xt
o as in ***oh***

Sometimes the vowel sounds are long. In hiragana, these long sounds are indicated by the addition of あ, い, う, え or お following the vowel. For instance, both the first and second vowel sounds in "Tokyo" are long, as the Japanese capital is actually closer to a four-syllable word in Japanese than the three-syllable word it has become in English. Thus, in hiragana, Tokyo is written とうきょう, with each う indicating an extended "o" sound.

In katakana, these elongated vowels are indicated by a long dash. The word "cheerleader," for example, is written チアリーダー, with the dashes elongating the "ri" and "da" sounds to match the Japanese pronunciation of "leader."

There are different ways to indicate the elongated vowels in romaji. For hiragana, this book uses a modified version of the Hepburn system: Long vowels indicated by an additional い or あ are romanized as ii and aa, respectively, but those featuring an additional う, え or お are romanized with just a single u, e or o.

It is highly unusual to use Hepburn romanization for katakana. Instead, the actual foreign spelling of the word is usually used. For instance, the word トイレットペーパー is simply "toilet paper" when romanized. But we need to work on our pronunciation as we learn katakana, so we're also going to include an unorthodox form of romanization. As a result, トイレットペーパー becomes not only "toilet paper," but also "toirettopeepaa." This type of romanization will look downright weird to those familiar with romaji, so don't get used to it. In fact, once you've learned kana, you should avoid romaji altogether – you won't need it anymore anyway!

Consonant sounds are virtually the same as those heard in English, with the

following exceptions. The "f" sound is considerably softer in Japanese than in English. And the "l" sound, of course, is almost nonexistent in Japanese, with a Japanese approximation falling somewhere between a "d" and an "r" to English-trained ears, and usually romanized with an "r."

Both hiragana and katakana make use of diacritic symbols called dakuten and handakuten to change the sounds of consonants. These modified characters are included in the charts at the front and back of this book.

A dakuten looks like this ゛ and turns k into g, t into d, s into z and h into b.

A handakuten looks like this ゜ and is used almost exclusively to turn h into p.

And a small っ (for hiragana) or ッ (for katakana) placed before a character doubles the consonant. For example, "kippu" (the Japanese word for ticket), is written as きっぷ in hiragana, while the English word "knock" (nokku in romaji) is written as ノック in katakana.

Finally, remember that all Japanese words end either in a vowel, or a consonant that can sound like either an "m" or an "n," depending on the word. This consonant is represented in hiragana as ん and in katakana as ン. There are no other consonant endings in Japanese.

STROKE ORDER

Now we're almost ready to start writing our kana, but it's important to learn the proper stroke order. This is essential to Japanese penmanship. Characters written using the wrong stroke order tend to look sloppy to trained eyes – and soon, your eyes will be able to tell the difference as well.

"Kana de Manga" makes this easy: At the bottom of each page is a practice area with numbered arrows indicating the sequence and direction of each stroke. In general, strokes are written from top to bottom, and left to right, with horizontal strokes followed by vertical strokes. Let's take a look at the hiragana character ま:

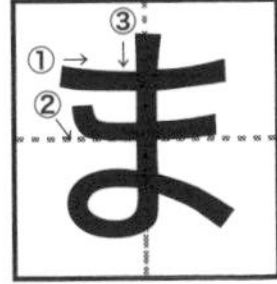

Here, the first stroke goes from left to right, the second goes a bit down before sweeping from left to right, and the final stroke goes straight down before looping up and around from the left. Top to bottom, left to right, horizontal before vertical.

Some kana are written in a single stroke that may change directions several times. These are among the easiest to write. A good example of this is the hiragana character る:

The stroke begins at the upper left and climbs slightly to the right before angling down in a long stroke to the left, then circling down toward the right and back to the left before looping again to the right. Single-stroke kana are among the easiest to write.

Multi-stroke kana may include a stroke that changes directions several times, like the hiragana character ね:

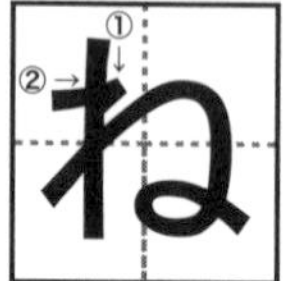

The first stroke is a straight line going from top to bottom. The second stroke juts from the left to the right before entering a sharp angle downward to the left, then sweeping back up to the right and down again, finishing in a loop that circles from left to right.

Katakana characters consist mainly of straight, angled strokes, and thus are very easy to memorize and write. Even the four-stroke character ネ is fairly simple:

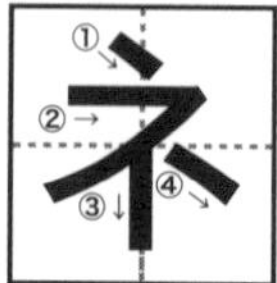

The first stroke is a short, angled line moving from left to right. The next stroke goes horizontally from left to right before reversing into a downward angle to the left. The third stroke travels down from the second, while the fourth moves in the same direction as the first.

There is much more to the use of hiragana and katakana than what we've just explained, of course. You can study Japanese for years, and still find new things to learn. The goal of "Kana de Manga" is simple: to introduce you to hiragana and katakana, help familiarize you with Japanese writing, and have a little fun doing it.

それでは、はじめましょう！ (Sore dewa, hajimemasho! So, let's begin!)

HIRAGANA AND KATAKANA

あしあと

***a*shiato**

footprints

If you really want to learn how to read and write Japanese, you're going to have to get your feet wet. The first step is to study ひらがな (hiragana) and かたかな (katakana), which is what this book will help you do. Take your time and don't get frustrated if you stumble now and then. Oh, and watch out for that puddle of mud!

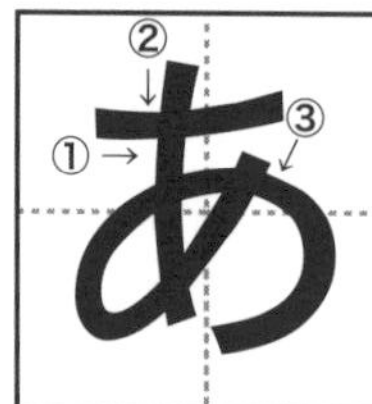

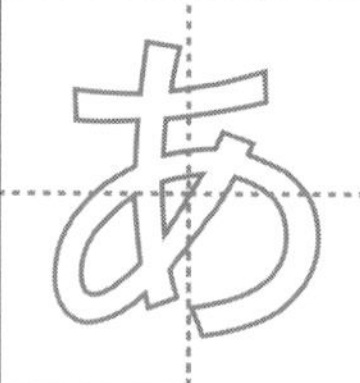

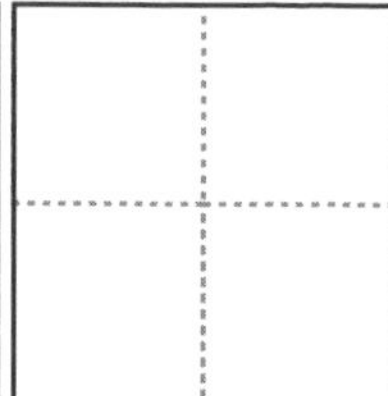

アルファベット

*a*rufuabetto

alphabet

Remember how easy it was to learn the ABCs when you were a child? Well, memorizing kana is just as simple! Invent word games, make flash cards, and perhaps even write a "kana song." Keep at it, and soon you too will be ぺらぺら (perapera; fluent) in Japanese.

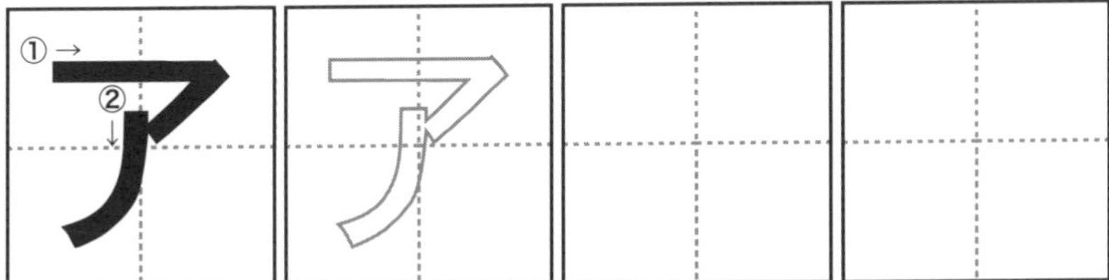

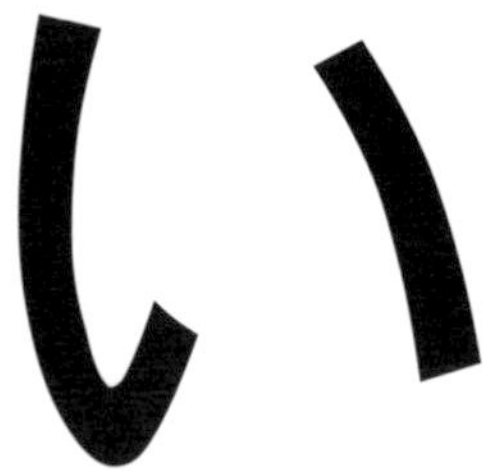

いそぐ

***i*sogu**

to hurry

Hey, buddy, what's the rush? Have you already memorized the first two かな (kana) characters in this book? No? Then turn back the page and work on あ and ア before you get too far ahead of yourself! Don't worry, we'll still be here when you catch up.

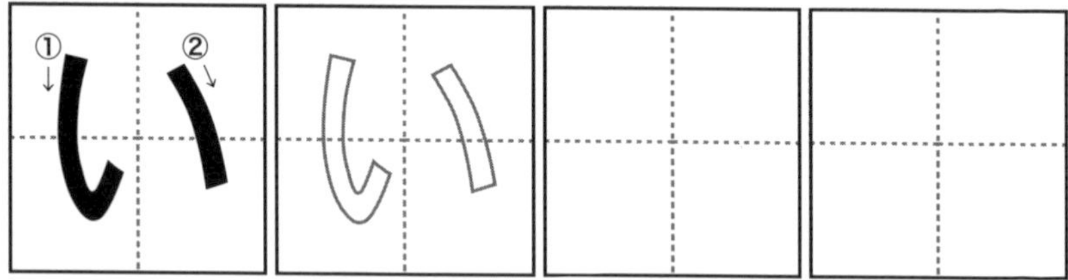

イヤリング

***i*yaringu**

earring

If diamonds really are a girl's best friend, then a lost earring is quite possibly her worst enemy, especially when she's already running late for a date. When she finally finds the elusive item, she is likely to shout あった (atta; there it is). The Japanese word for "lost item" is おとしもの (otoshimono).

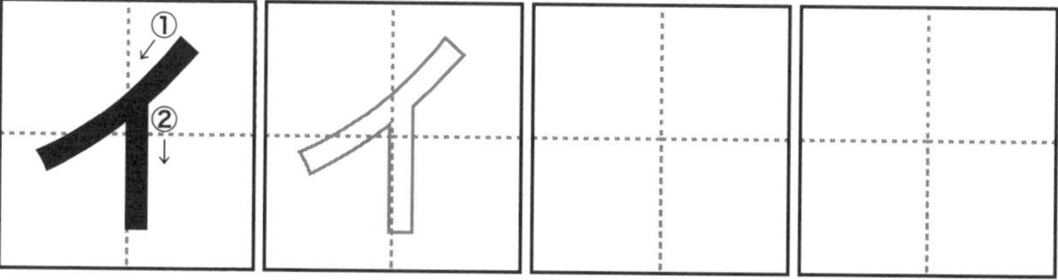

umi

beach, sea

Nobody said that learning にほんご (nihongo; Japanese) would be a day at the beach, but it's still lots of fun! And here's an interesting fact: Japan is a しょとう (shoto; chain of islands) with more than 18,000 miles of coastline. That's enough room for one big beach bash!

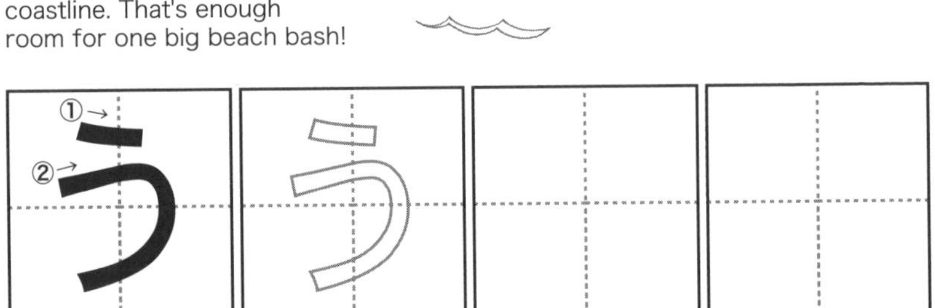

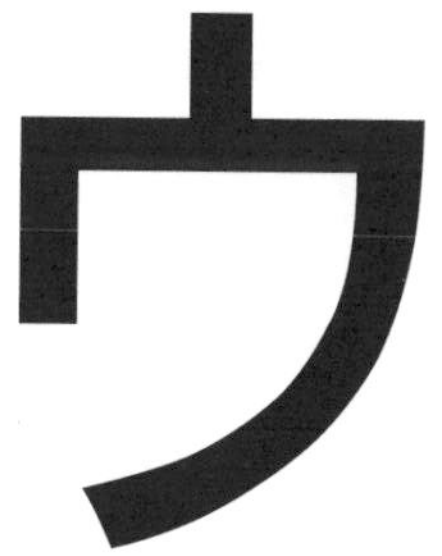

ウインク

***u*inku**

wink

A wink is worth a thousand words—especially when it's made by a びしょうじょ (bishojo; beautiful girl). The guy pictured here, though, seems to be a bit はずかしい (hazukashii; embarrassed) by his flirtatious friend.

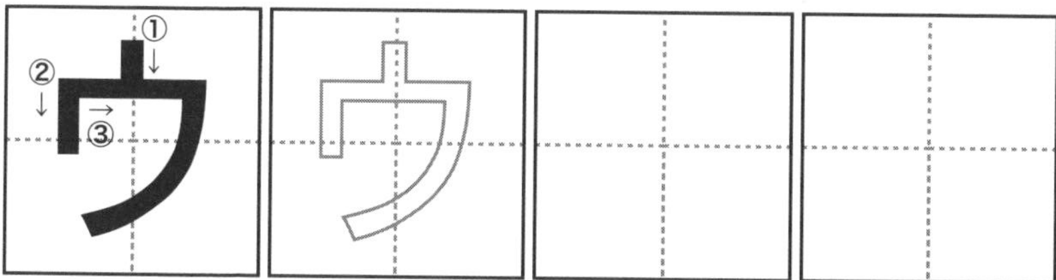

えほん

ehon

picture book

Parents in Japan read to their children many of the same fairy tales enjoyed by toddlers in North America and Europe, including シンデレラものがたり (Shinderera Monogatari), better known as "The Story of Cinderella." Of course, the Japanese have their own folk stories, including the curiously titled ももたろう (Momotaro), or "Peach Boy."

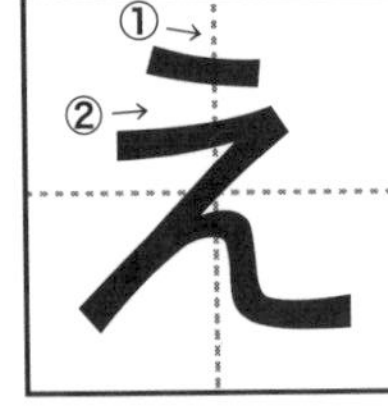

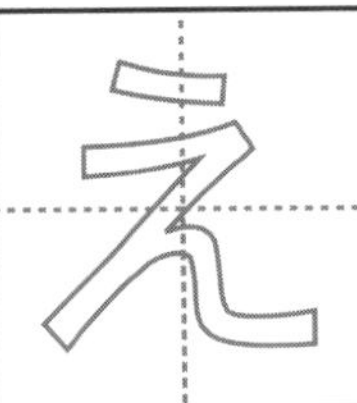

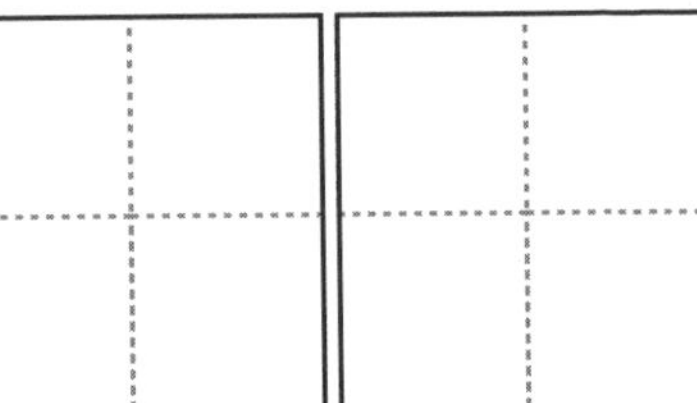

エラー

*e*ra

error

The Great American Pastime is also a hit in Japan, where やきゅう (yakyu; baseball) is played year-round. High school tournaments are held twice a year at Koushien Stadium and televised nationwide, with virtually every household in the country tuned in. It's the last place a player wants to misjudge a ground ball.

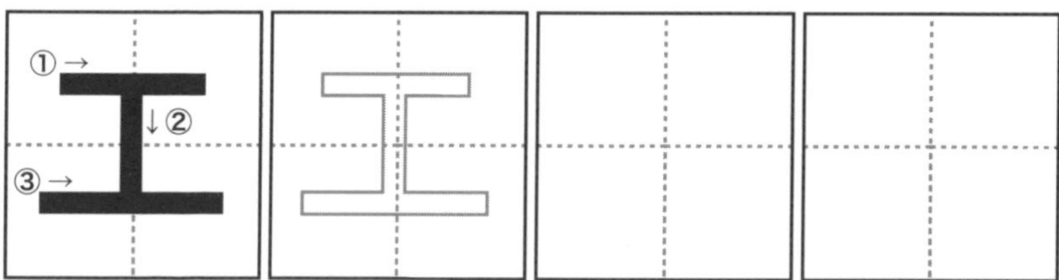

おんせん

***o**nsen*

hot spring

Among Japan's most popular tourist attractions are hot-spring resorts where wild さる (saru; monkeys) soak with the tourists. It's usually a very calm and pleasant experience. However, once in a while the monkeys go bananas and attack their guests. So, if you ever visit one of these places, bathe at your own risk!

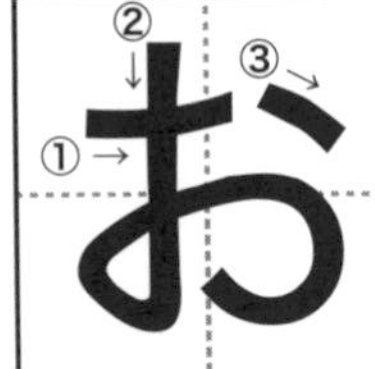

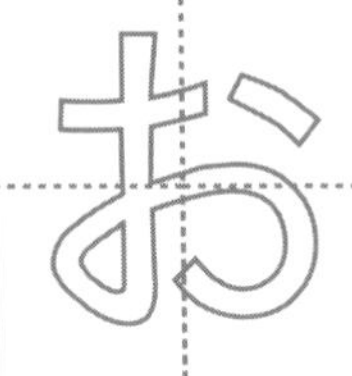

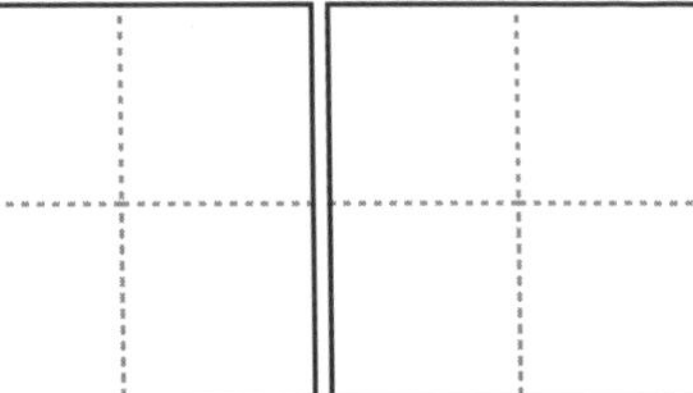

オルゴール

***o**rugoru*

music box

Orgel, the Dutch (and German) word for organ, becomes オルゴール in Japanese, and is used to describe all types of music boxes, from simple jewelry containers to elaborate musical figurines from 19th-century ヨーロッパ (Yoroppa; Europe).

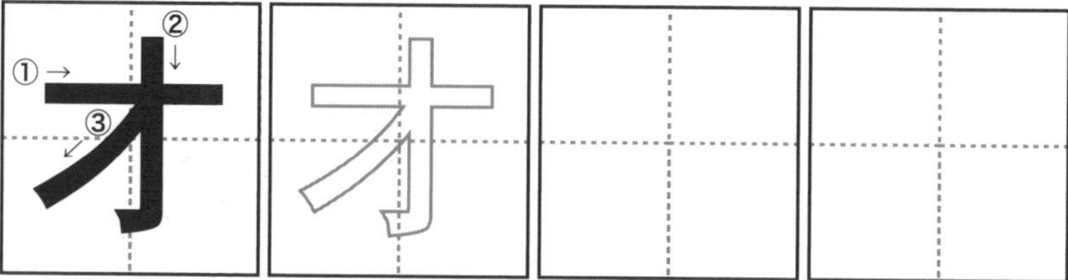

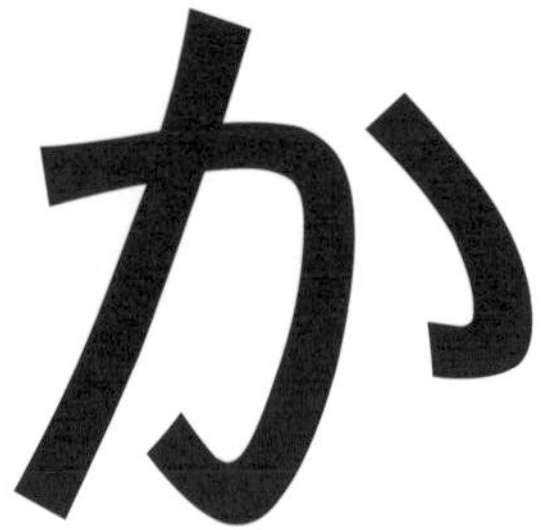

か

ka

mosquito

Planning a summertime trip to Japan? Be sure to have plenty of mosquito-repellant on hand! The pesky insects are everywhere, and they're always hungry! Fortunately, they are more an itch-inducing nuisance than anything else, and there is no risk of マラリア (mararia; malaria) in Japan.

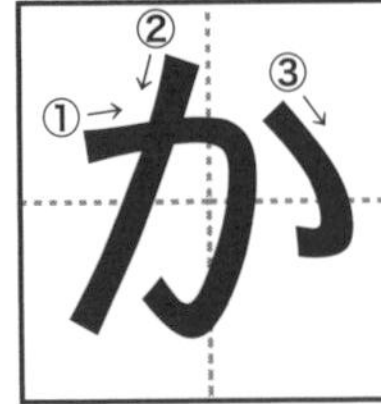

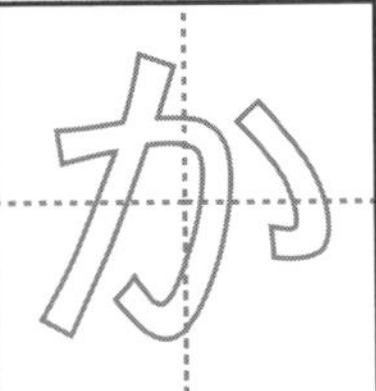

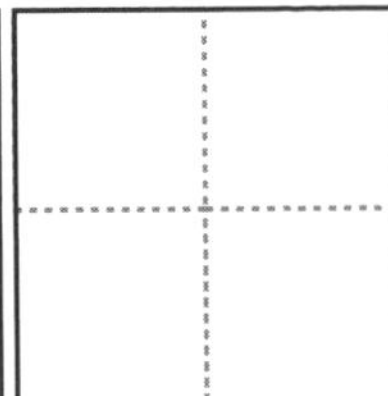

カラオケ

***ka*raoke**

karaoke

In Japan, everyone wants to be a singer. That explains the popularity of karaoke clubs, where would-be rock 'n' rollers gather to give their vocal cords a workout. Few, however, have the stuff it takes to become a star, and their audiences (usually consisting of close friends) often leave the clubs screaming みみがいたい (mimi ga itai; my ears hurt)!

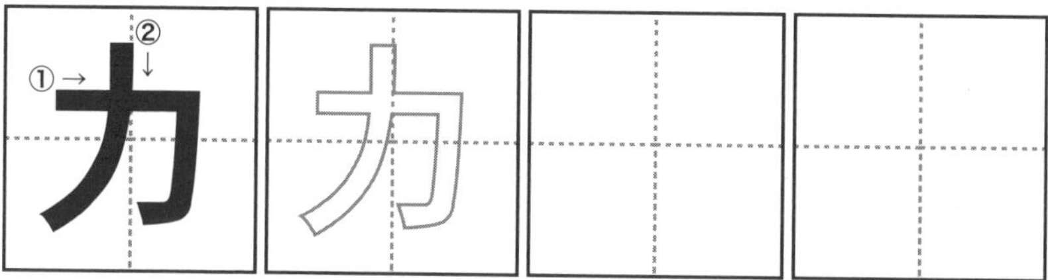

きもの

***ki*mono**

kimono

Meet the Tone Twins, リナちゃん (Rina-chan) and サキちゃん (Saki-chan). In addition to sharing the same birthday, these two fun-loving sisters from Tokyo attend the same school (Manga University, of course), shop at the same stores, and sometimes even date the same guys!
They also share a keen sense of style, especially when it comes to Japanese kimono. Rina favors the refined look of earth-tone silk, while Saki prefers bright floral patterns. Lucky for us—otherwise, it would be impossible to tell them apart!

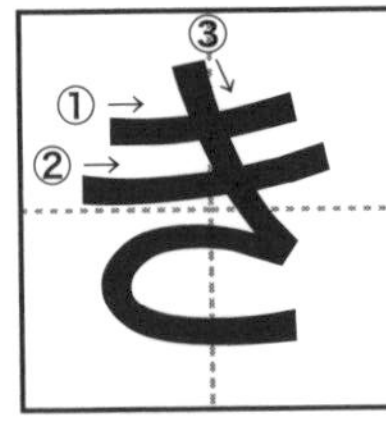

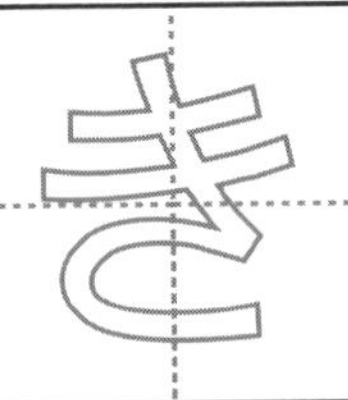

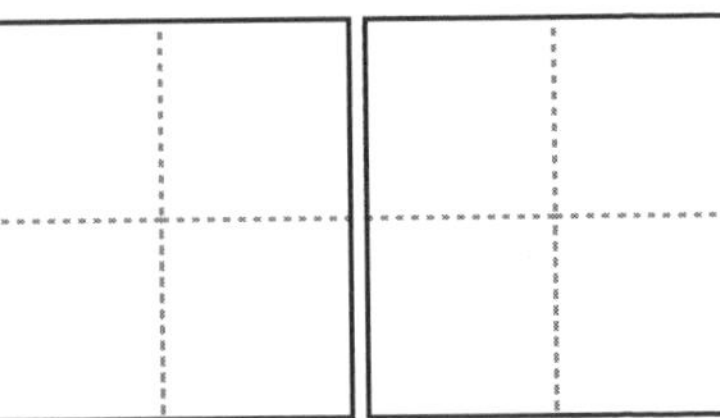

キノコ

***ki*noko**

mushroom

The names of plants and animals are often written in katakana, though hiragana is also used. Mushroom, for instance, can be written as either キノコ or きのこ. We like 'em both ... especially on top of ピザ (piza; pizza).

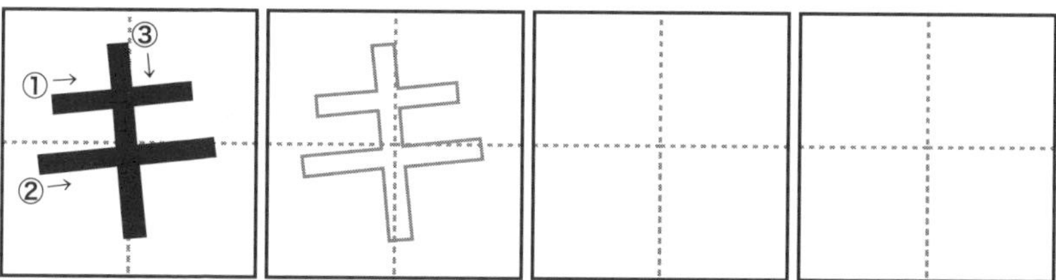

kutsu

shoes

There's nothing that makes a little guy feel like a big man more than walking around in his daddy's shoes. Let's just hope he remembers to take them off before stepping foot into a Japanese home, though, where wearing shoes is だめ (dame), a no-no.

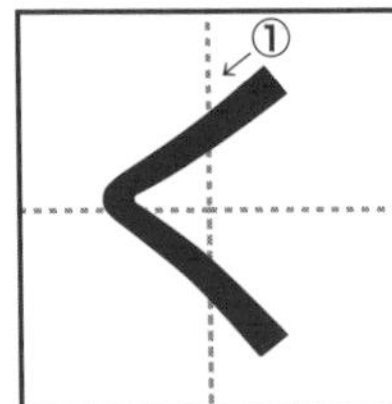

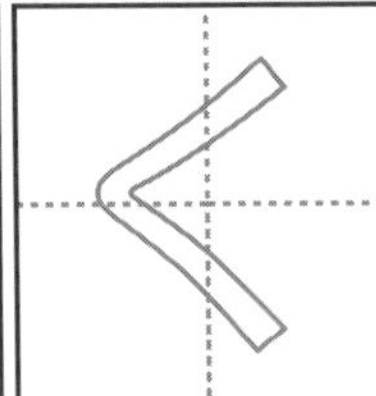

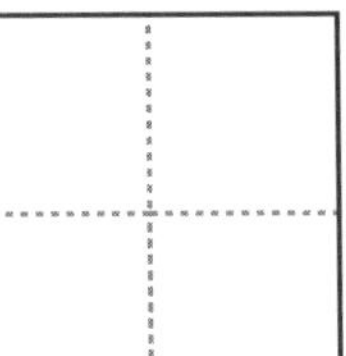

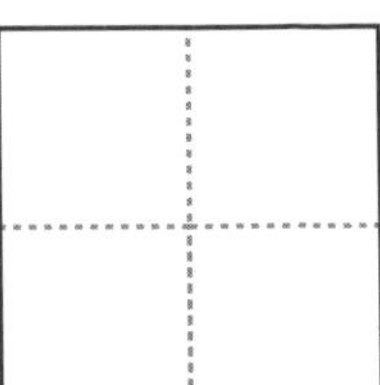

クジラ

***ku**jira*

whale

Japan is one of the few nations of the world to practice the hunting of whales despite a worldwide ban on the activity. However, there is a significant animal-rights movement in the country that is trying to get the government to change its policy and protect the ぜつめつきぐしゅ (zetsumetsukigushu; endangered species).

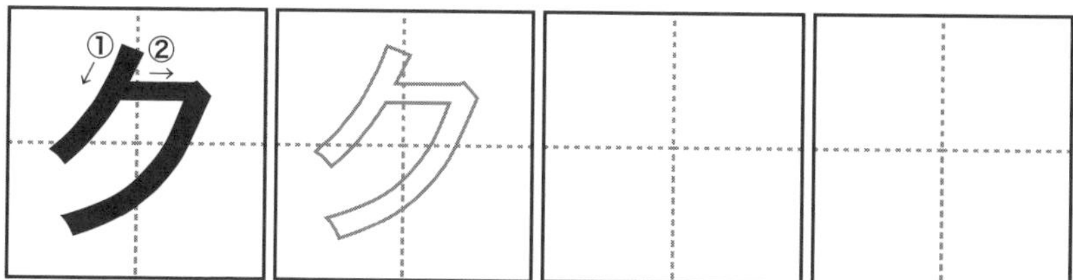

けいたいでんわ

***ke**taidenwa*

cellular phone

Although convenient and easy to use, cellular phones are also the source of much irritation in Japan. For instance, there's nothing more frustrating to a young guy than when he gives his でんわばんごう (denwabango; phone number), to a pretty girl he meets at a party, and she never calls him back!

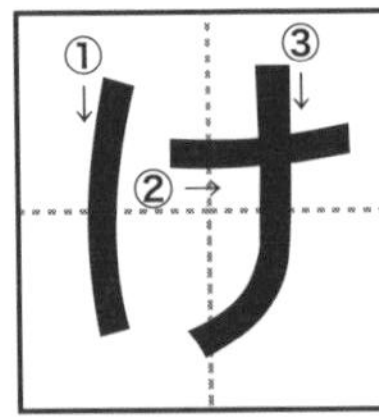

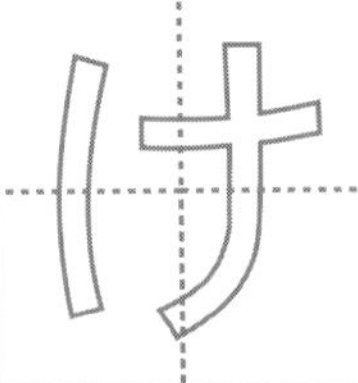

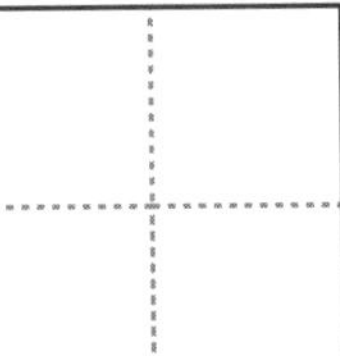

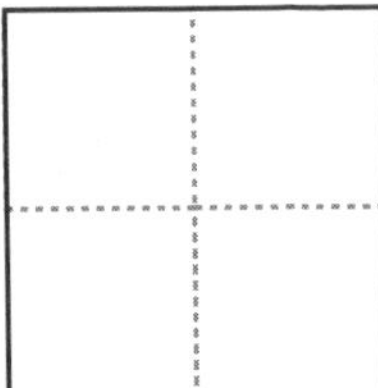

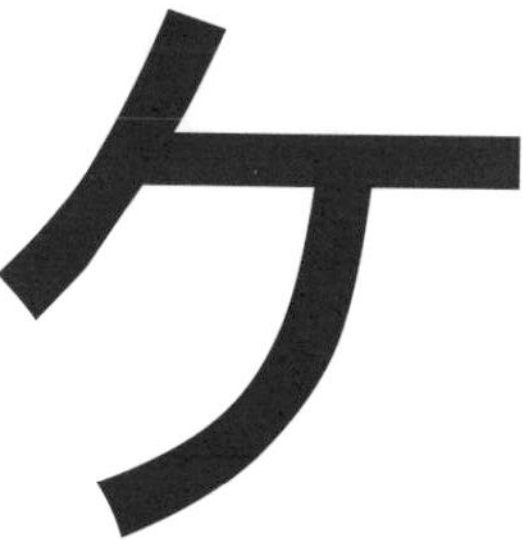

ケーキ

***ke*ki**

cake

Now we know why the pretty girl never called our ともだち (tomodachi; friend) on the previous page. She's already involved in a long-term relationship ... with the bakery-next-door!

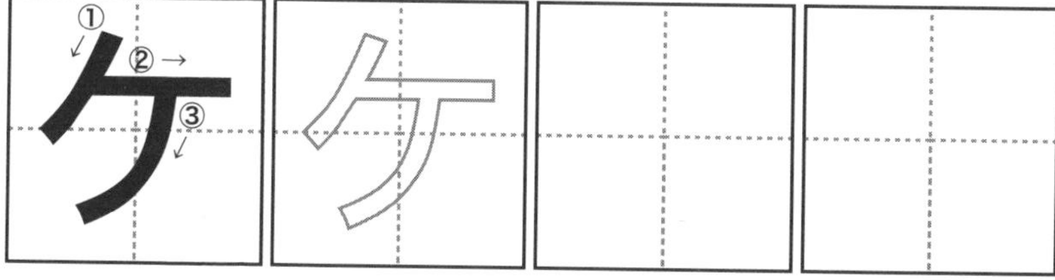

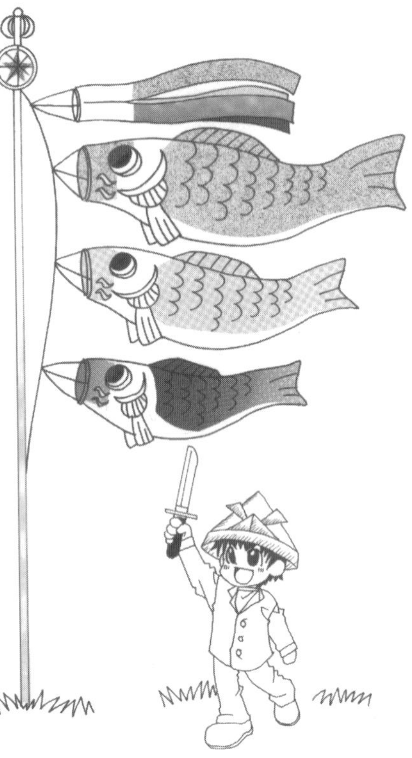

こいのぼり

***ko**inobori*

carp-shaped streamer

To the Japanese, the こい (koi; carp), is a symbol of courage and strength, traits they hope to instill in their sons. So, during the weeks leading up to the こどものひ (Kodomo no Hi; Children's Day) holiday in May, parents proudly display carp-shaped のぼり (nobori; streamers) outside their homes to honor their sons. The colorful windsocks are a remarkable sight to behold, and one of the enduring memories of a springtime trip to Japan.

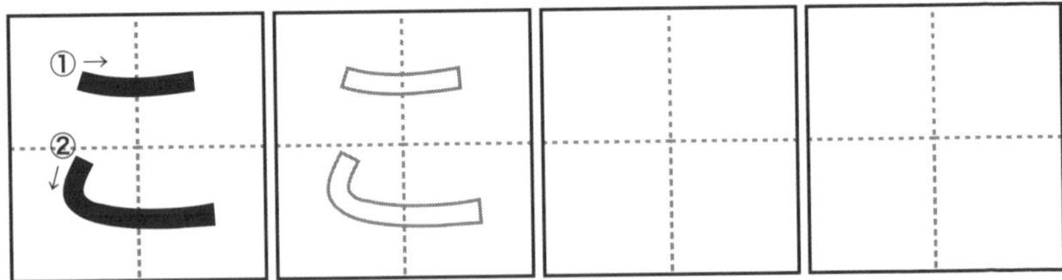

コアラ

***ko**ara*

koala bear

There aren't any koala bears in Japan (except for those in zoos), but there are plenty of koala cookies. コアラのマーチ (Koara no Maachi; March of the Koalas), is a popular brand of chocolate-filled biscuits shaped like tiny koala bears. Absolutely おいしい (oishii; delicious)!

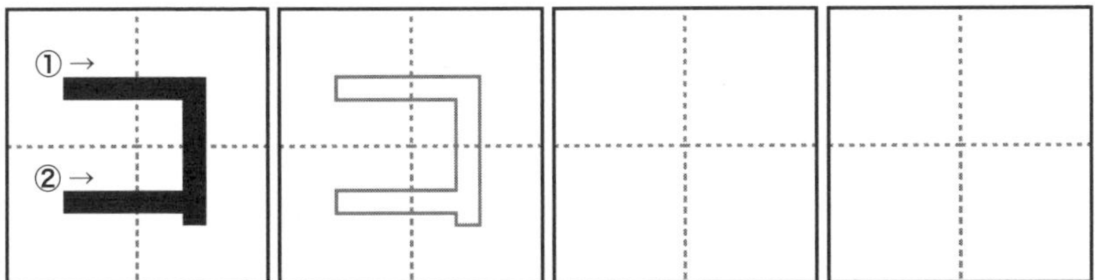

さむい

***sa**mui*

cold

If you've never been to Japan, you might not be aware that the country's northernmost main island, Hokkaido, is one of the coldest places on Earth, with winter temperatures falling well below freezing. Hokkaido is also the home of the あいぬ (Ainu), Japan's indigenous people. The word Ainu means "human."

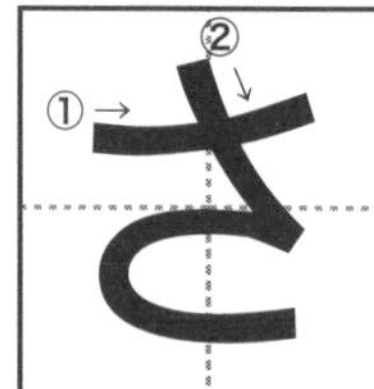

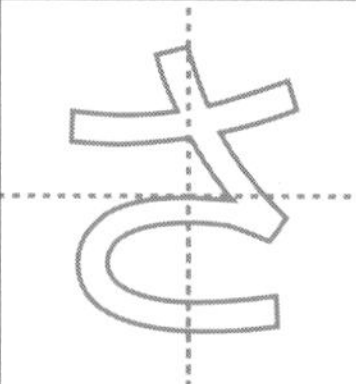

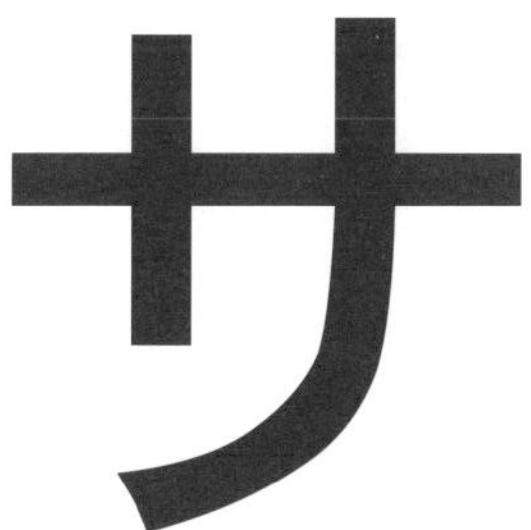

サラリーマン

***sa**rariiman*

salaryman

(businessman)

Pity the poor Japanese salaryman. His ぶちょう (bucho; boss) makes him work late into the night, he hasn't had a vacation in nearly 10 years, and now Mother Nature has blown his cover. Time to buy a new かつら (katsura; wig).

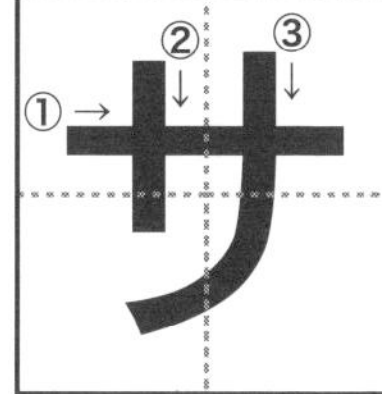

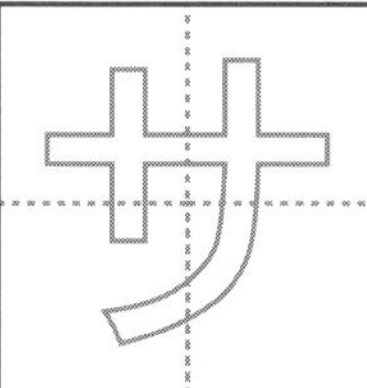

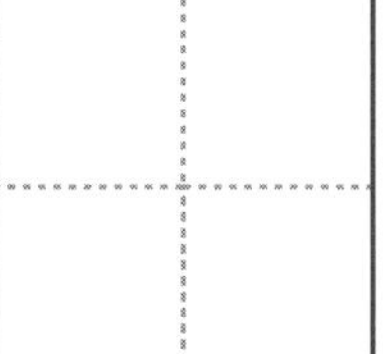

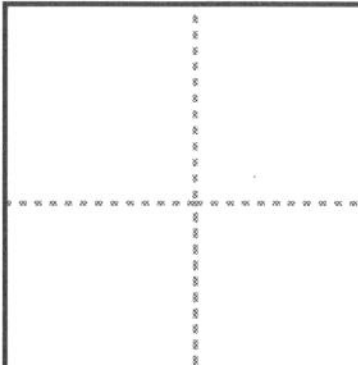

した

***shi*ta**

tongue

Sticking your tongue out at someone is rude in any culture. We have a feeling, though, that this kid has a problem keeping his tongue inside his big くち (kuchi; mouth).

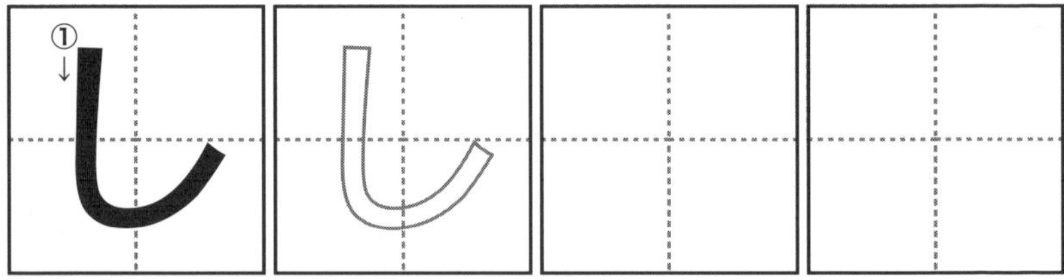

シール

***shii*ru**

seal

(sticker)

You'd think that playing with stickers would be a harmless activity. Not true, though, if おかあさん (okaasan; mom) just finished ぞうきんかけ (zokinkake; mopping the floor)!

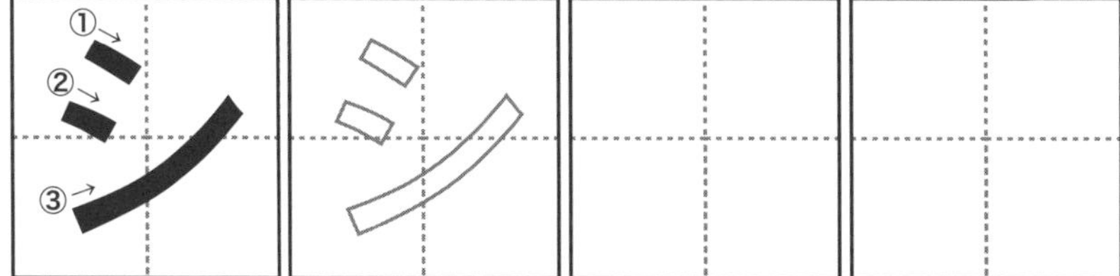

す

すもう

***su**mo*

sumo

The ancient Japanese sport of sumo wrestling features some of the strongest—and largest—men in the world. One sumo superstar, the Hawaiian-born Konishiki, weighed more than 600 pounds at one point during his career!

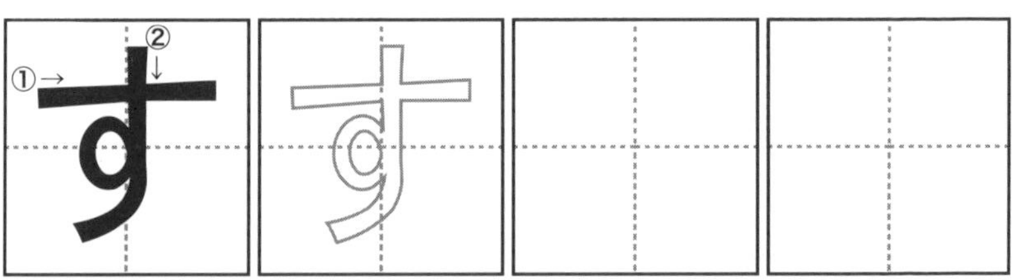

①→ ②↓ す

スイカ

suika

watermelon

Summertime is suika time in Japan, and kids flock to the beach to play スイカわり (suikawari), a game whose object is to split open a watermelon with a heavy stick while blindfolded. Similar to a Mexican pinata party ... but messier!

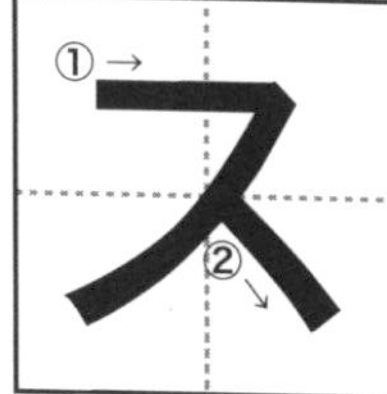

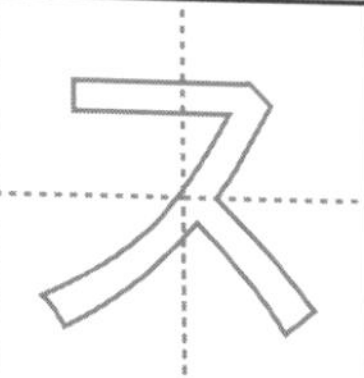

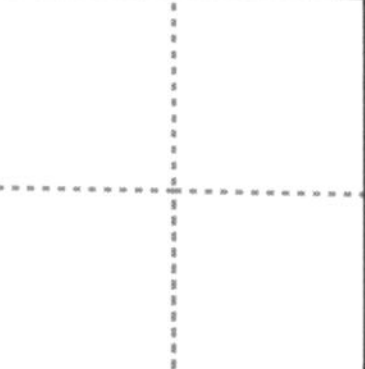

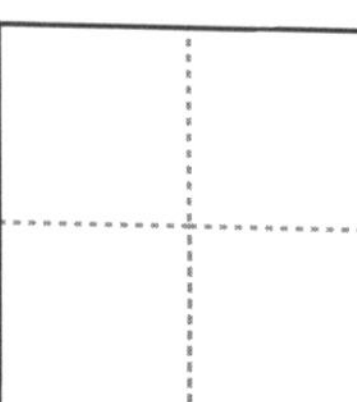

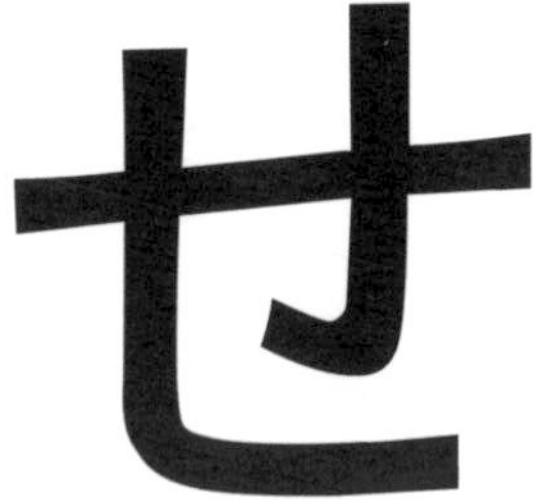

せいふく

***se**ifuku*

school uniform

By adding such things as designer scarves and ルーズソックス (ruuzu sokkusu; loose socks), girls have transformed their traditional school uniforms into ultra-chic fashion statements. せいふく is actually a shortened form of がくせいふく (gakuseifuku), which combines the words がくせい (gakusei; student) and ふく (fuku; clothes).

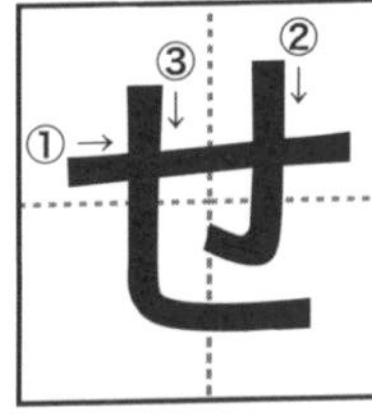

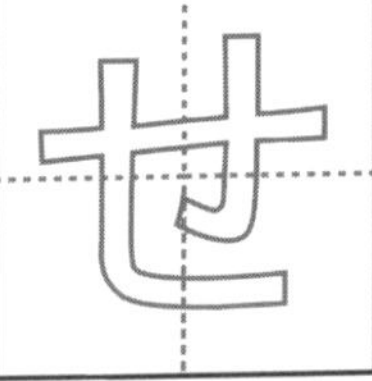

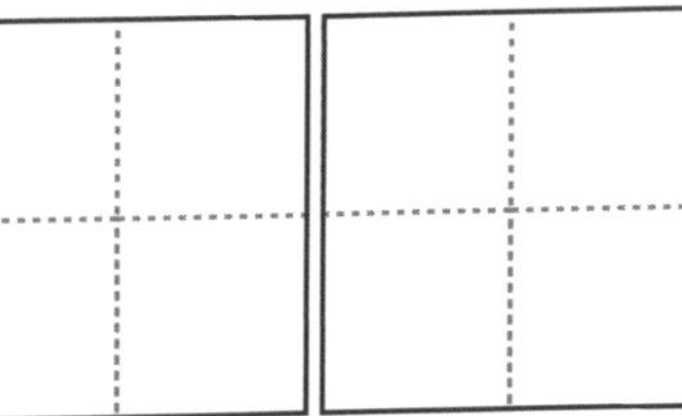

*se*etaa

sweater

Another fashionable addition to the traditional school uniform is an おおきすぎる (okisugiru; oversized) sweater. Perfect for keeping the chill out during the bitterly cold ふゆ (fuyu; winter).

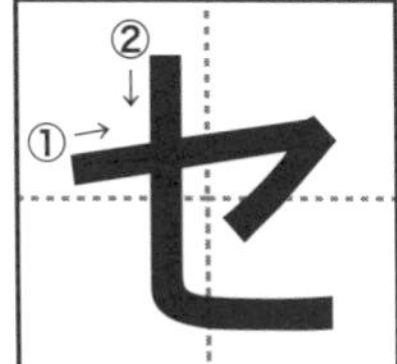

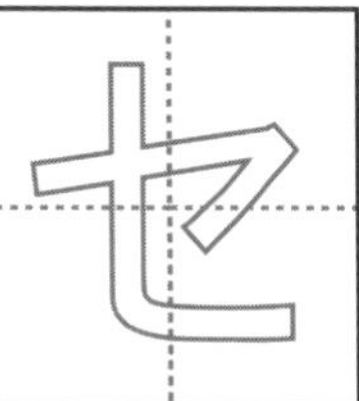

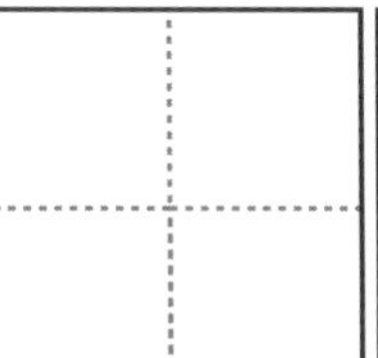

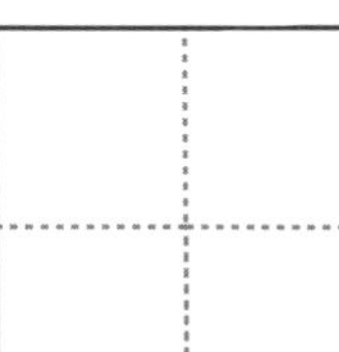

そつぎょう

***so**tsugyo*

graduation

Ceremonies are held for graduating students at all levels of education in Japan, from preschool through college. However, equally important to the Japanese are にゅうがくしき (nyugakushiki), formal daylong events held when students enter school for the first time.

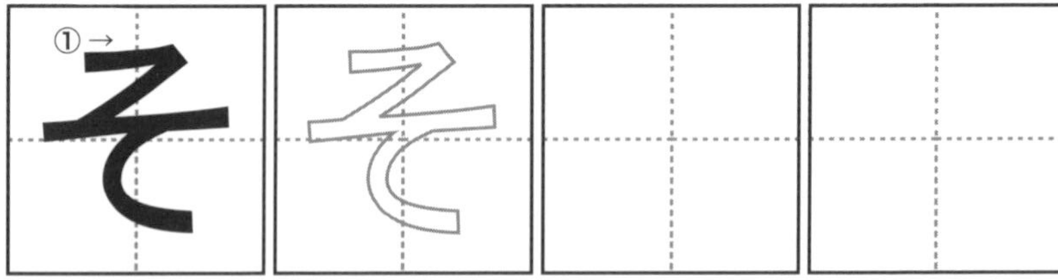

ソックス

***so*kkusu**

socks

Having a hole in your socks is nothing to be embarrassed about—unless you're inside a friend's いえ (ie; house) where shoes are not permitted. The traditional word for socks is くつした (kutsushita), which combines くつ (kutsu; shoes) and した (shita; below). The katakana form, however, is also widely used.

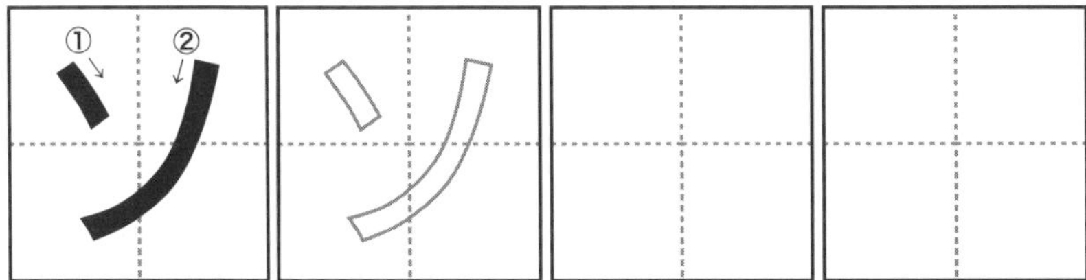

たからもの

***ta**karamono*

treasure

This word combines たから (takara; treasure) with もの (mono; things), to become "treasure things." Many other common nouns also end with もの. For instance, たべもの (tabemono; eating things, or food); のりもの (norimono; riding things, or vehicles); and わすれもの (wasuremono; lost/forgotten things).

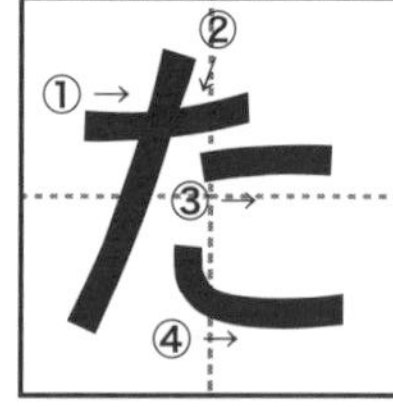

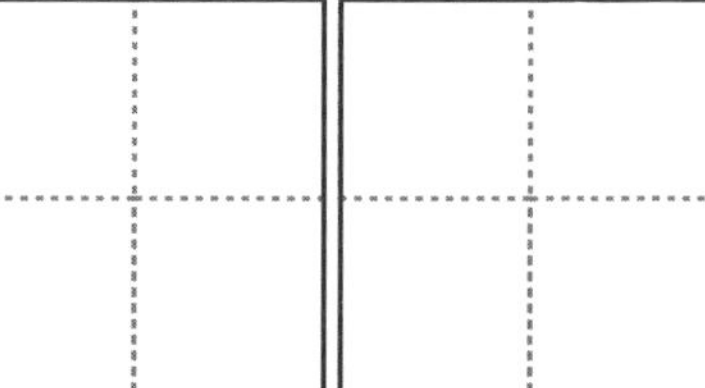

ターバン

***taa**ban*

turban

There are several species of へび (hebi; snakes) indigenous to Japan, but へびつかい (hebitsukai; snake charmers) hail from インド (Indo; India), of course.

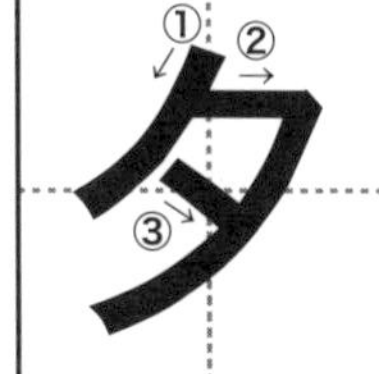

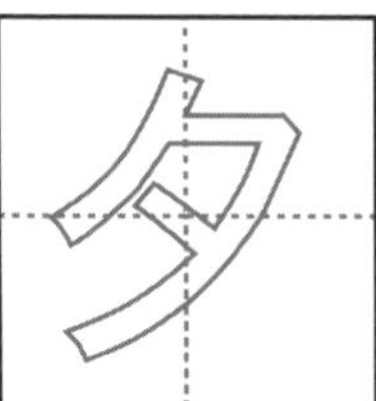

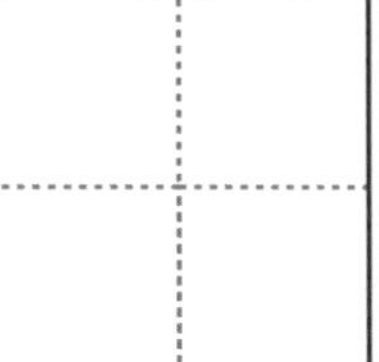

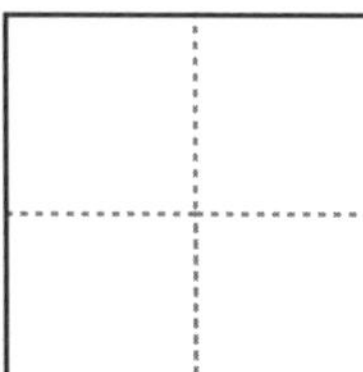

ち

chi

blood

It may only be a little scratch, but try telling that to this おとこのこ (otoko no ko; boy). Judging by the look on his face, it's safe to assume he's just a wee bit squeamish when it comes to seeing his own blood. Ouch!

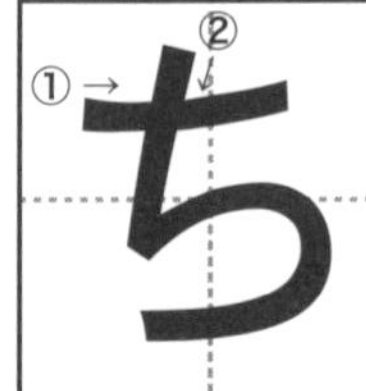

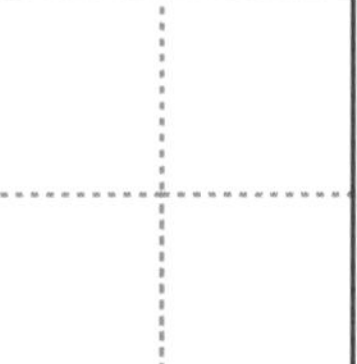

チアリーダー

chiariidaa

cheerleader

Gimme a ゴー! Gimme a チー! Gimme a ム! Gimme another ゴー! What does it spell? ゴーチームゴー (Go chiimu go; Go team, go)! OK, that was silly. But making up your own cheerleader chants using hiragana and katakana really is a great way to memorize the characters.

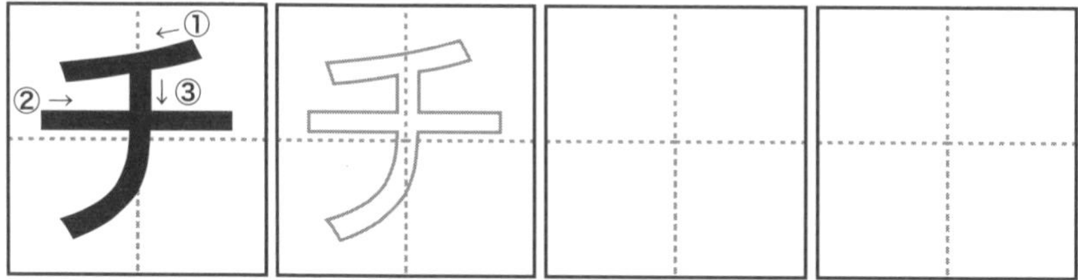

つき

***tsu*ki**

moon

The myth of the "the man in the moon" is well-known in North America and Europe. However, the Japanese take on this lunar legend is a bit different. Rather than the face of a man, they see the image of an うさぎ (usagi; rabbit) making もち (mochi; rice cakes).

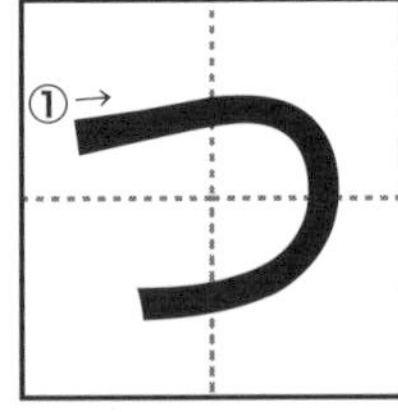

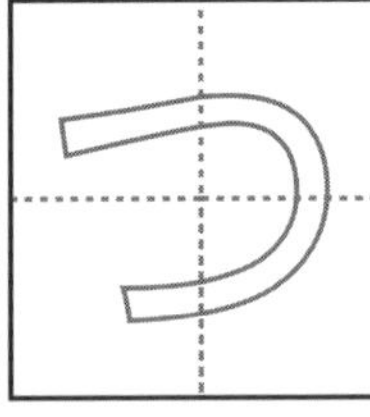

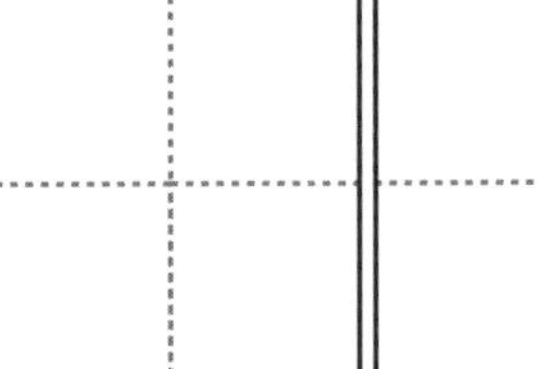

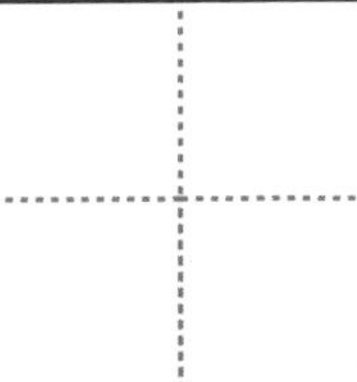

ツーショット

***tsuu**shotto*

two-shot

(photograph of a couple)

Many young Japanese couples enjoy taking photos together in what are called プリクラ (purikura; print clubs)—arcades with photograph vending machines that shoot and print images onto tiny stickers. The word プリクラ is a contraction of プリント (purinto; print) and クラブ (kurabu; club). はい、チーズ (Hai, chiizu; Say cheese)!

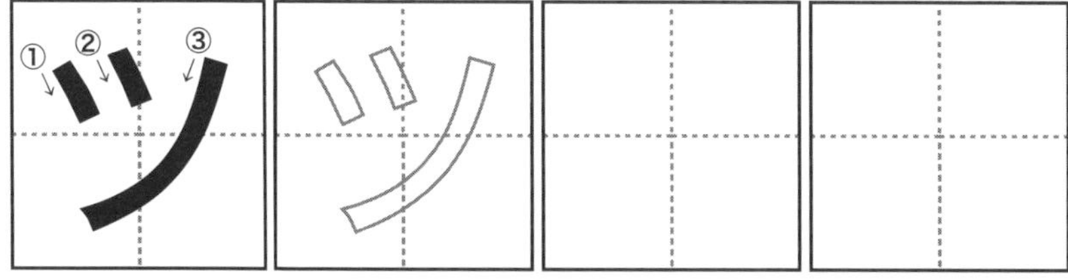

てじな

***te*jina**

magic

On its own, て (te) means "hand," and てじな quite literally translates as "sleight of hand." There are several ways to say "magician" in Japanese, including てじなし (tejinashi), which is also the word for "juggler," and マジシャン (majishan). And now watch as the magician pulls a rabbit out of her ぼうし (boshi; hat).

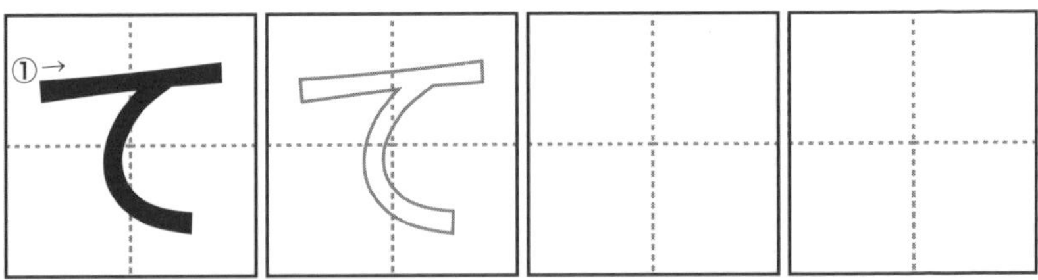

テスト

***te**suto*

test

The word "test" is a scary one in any language. Our friend here is worried he'll be denied the せんえん (senen; 1,000 yen) that mom has promised him if he gets a ごうかくてん (gokakuten; passing grade). He should have spent more time studying at the じゅく (juku; cram school).

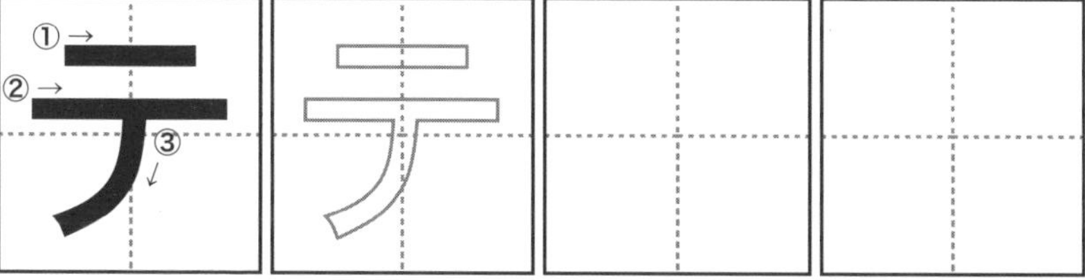

とんぼ

***to*nbo**

dragonfly

Japan's first emperor is said to have once remarked that the shape of the country resembled that of a dragonfly, a symbol of playfulness and strength. To this day, Japanese fondly refer to their country as あきつしま (Akitsushima; The Dragonfly Islands).

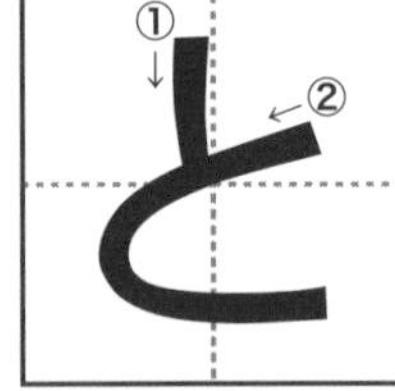

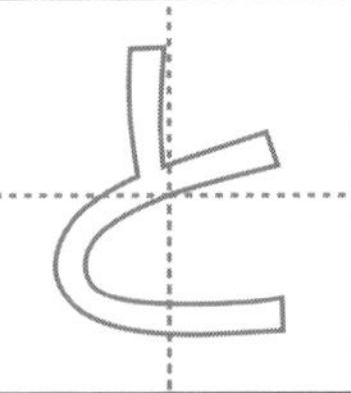

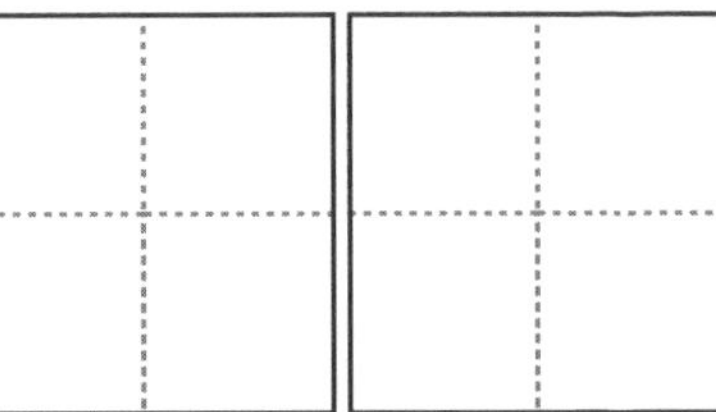

トイレット ペーパー

***to**irettopeipaa*

toilet paper

Bathroom tissue is usually intended for serious "business," but this あかちゃん (akachan; baby) has found a whole new use for the stuff. Another word for toilet paper is おとしがみ (otoshigami).

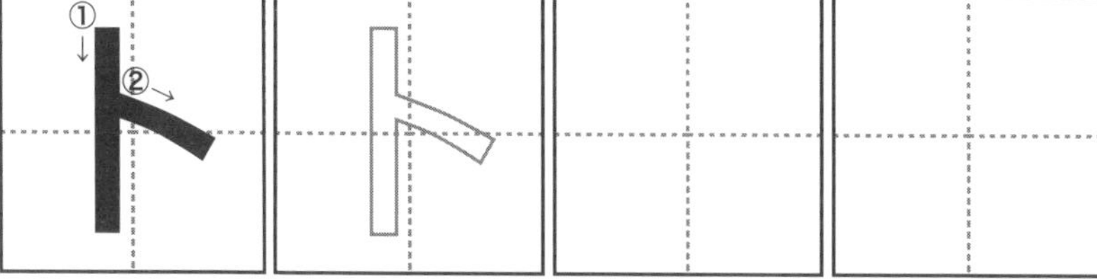

なきむし

***na**kimushi*

crybaby

Have you ever noticed that many アニメ(anime; Japanese cartoons) feature a main character who is always whining about something? Strange as it may seem, crybabies are often considered かわいい (kawaii; cute). Personally, we find them to be かわいそう (kawaiso; pathetic)!

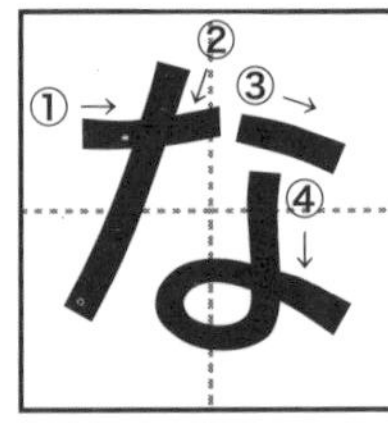

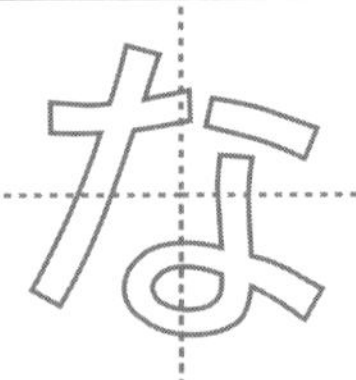

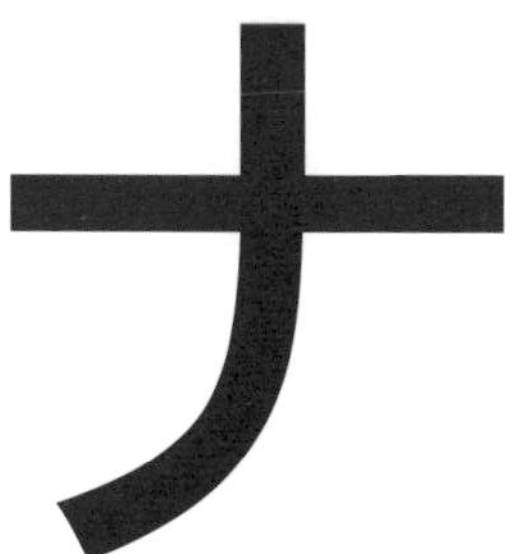

ナース

***naa**su*

nurse

"Trust me; this won't hurt a bit." How many times have you heard a nurse say that just before she sticks you with a foot-long needle? あぶないですよ (Abunai desu yo; Watch out)!

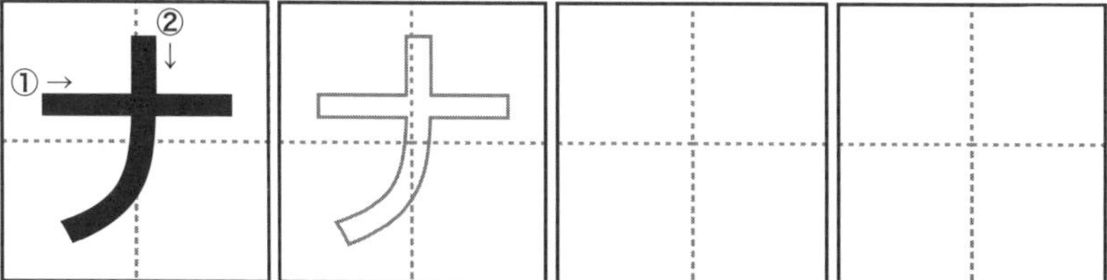

にんじゃ

***ni*nja**

ninja

Countless movies have been made about the ninja and their service as secret assassins in feudal Japan. Truth, however, really is stranger than fiction. For instance, most of these stealth warriors were originally farmers—not fighters—and many of them were devout followers of the しんとう (Shinto) religion. Their full history, however, remains shrouded in mystery.

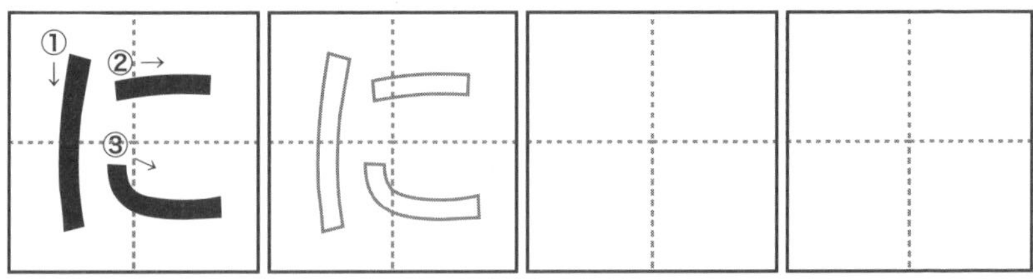

ニュース

***n*yuusu**

news

Watching Japanese news broadcasts on the テレビ (terebi; television) is another excellent way to improve your comprehension of the language. NHK, Japan's public broadcasting network, uses えいせいほうそう (eiseihoso; satellite broadcasts) to beam its newscasts to viewers throughout the world.

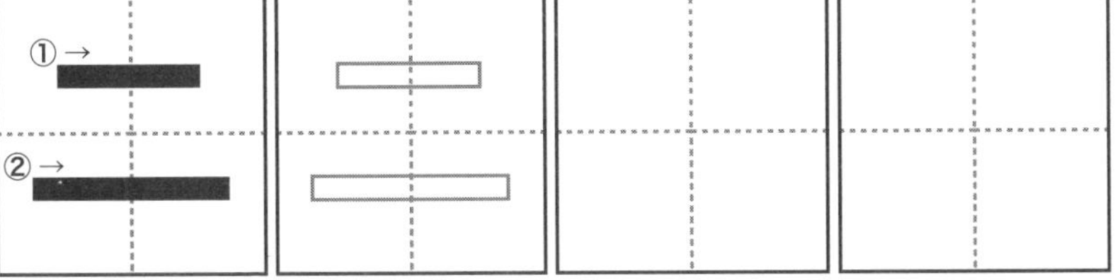

ぬれる

***nu**reru*

to get wet

If you've ever been in Japan during つゆ (tsuyu; the rainy season), you know the feeling of the poor guy pictured here. This miserable meteorological period usually begins in late May and continues well into July, when temperatures begin to soar and things get really むしあつい (mushiatsui; hot and humid).

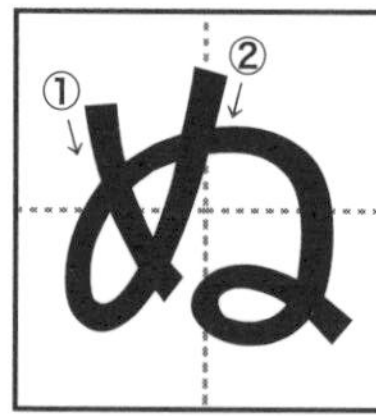

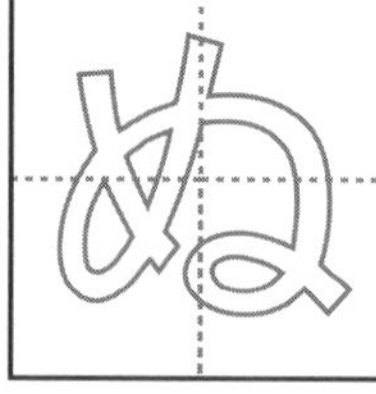

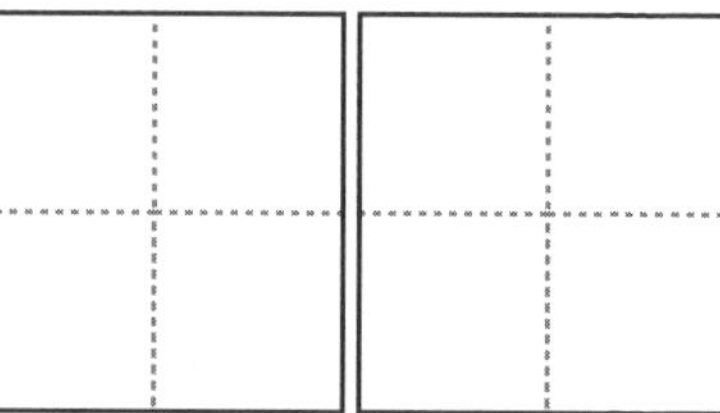

ヌンチャク

***nu**nchaku*

nunchaku

This well-known weapon is said to have originated in ancient Okinawa, a large island that lies about halfway between Japan (of which Okinawa is now a part) and Taiwan. Martial-arts historians believe the first nunchaku were used not as weapons but rather as some sort of farming tool. Another word for nunchaku is そせつこん (sosetsukon), though it is not as common.

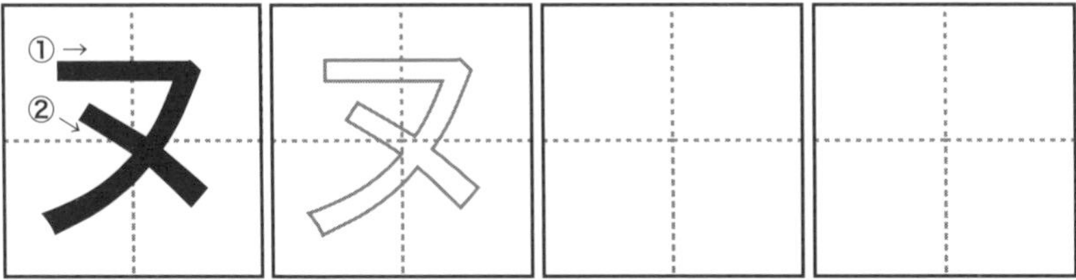

ねこ

***ne*ko**

cat

Nearly 8 million of Japan's cramped homes still manage to make room for pet cats. Ceramic feline figurines called まねきねこ (manekineko; beckoning cat) are kept as good-luck charms by nearly every business owner in the land. And Hello Kitty is a national icon. Make no doubt about it: Japan is the cat's meow.

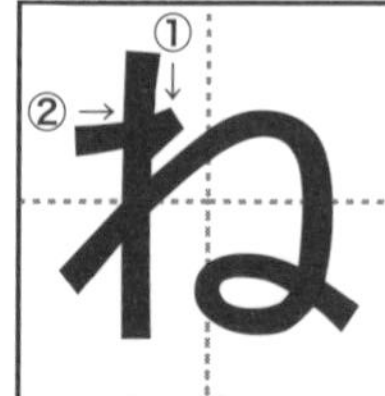

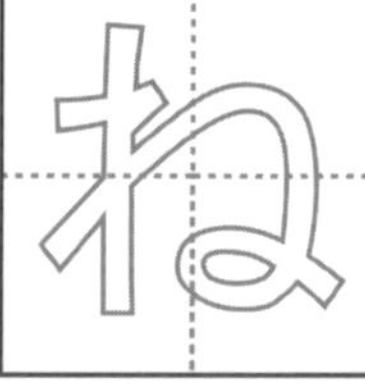

ネクタイ

***ne*kutai**

necktie

In nearly every Japanese オフィス (ofuisu; office), male employees are required to wear スーツ (suutsu; suits) and neckties. Dad may be a traditionalist, but we think the little guy has the right idea.

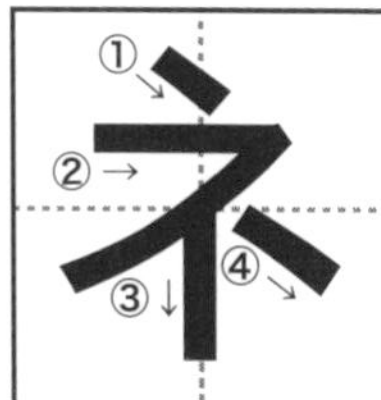

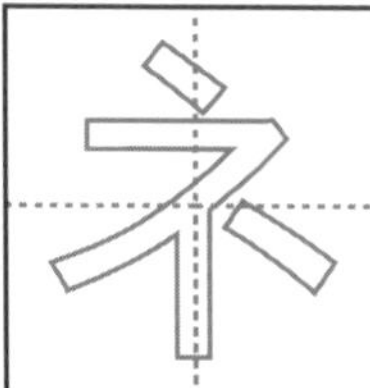

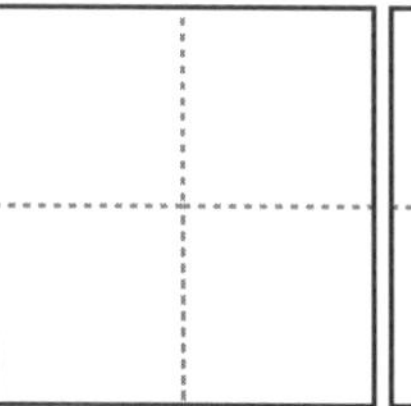

のっぺらぼう

***no**pperabo*

faceless female ghost

This expressionless apparition is one of Japan's most famous おばけ (obake; monsters). Legend has it that she haunts men who have harmed women. Many Japanese horror stories take place in summer during おぼん (obon; the Lantern Festival), when ghosts are said to return to their ancestral homes.

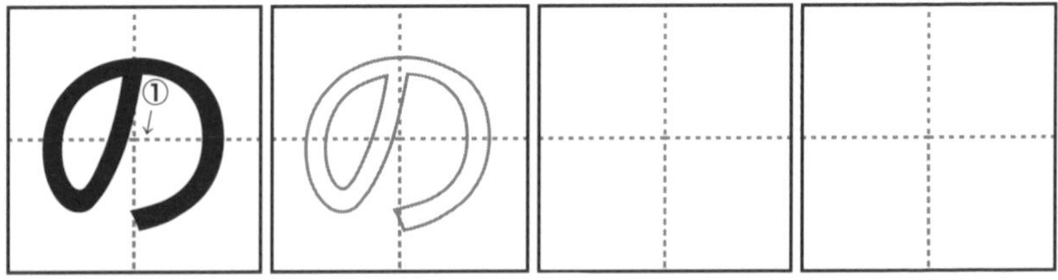

ノック

***no*kku**

knock

Many people in Japan keep the doors to their homes unlocked. So when a visitor arrives, rather than knocking, he or she will simply open the door and proclaim ごめんください (gomen kudasai), which means "Excuse me," "I'm here" or "May I come in?"

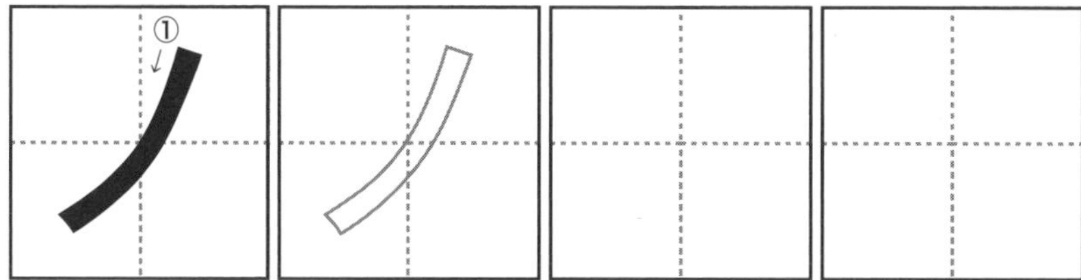

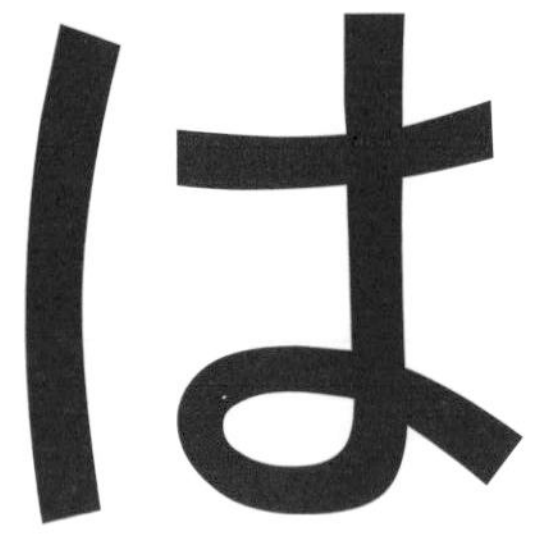

はな

***ha**na*

flower

Although Japan does not have an official national flower, the さくら (sakura; cherry blossom) certainly symbolizes the country. When the cherry trees are in full bloom (usually in late March), huge crowds gather in local parks for はなみ (hanami; flower viewing) parties. The きく (kiku; chrysanthemum) is also a Japanese favorite, and is used in the Imperial Family's crest.

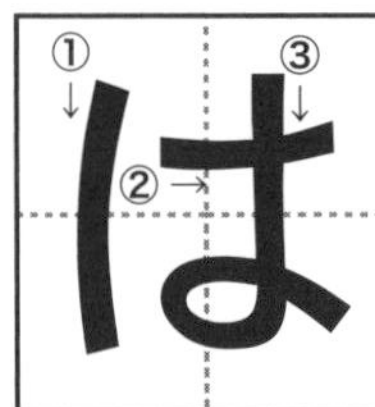

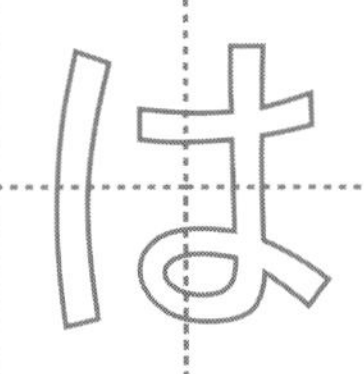

ハンバーガー

***ha**nbaagaa*

hamburger

Western-style restaurants abound in Japan, and hamburgers are always available. However, take care when placing your order. With the bun, it's a ハンバーガー (hanbaagaa); without the bun, it's called ハンバーグ (hanbaagu). Either way, we like it topped with チーズ (chiizu; cheese).

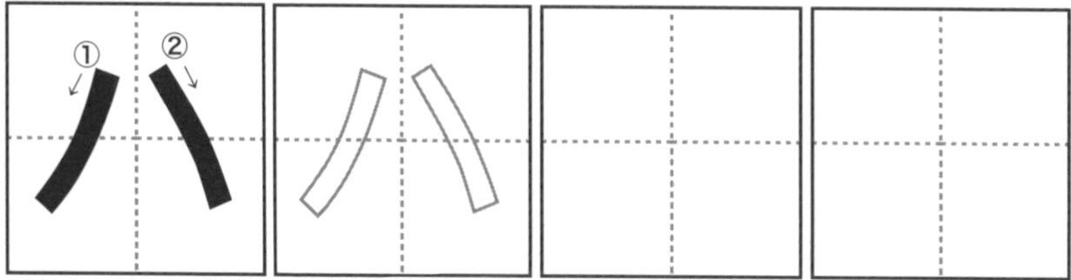

ひとめぼれ

***hi*tomebore**

love at first sight

It's a familiar scene: Boy sees girl, boy falls head-over-heels for girl, girl goes to the prom with the captain of the からて (karate) team instead. To paraphrase the French, しょうがない (shoganai; c'est la vie).

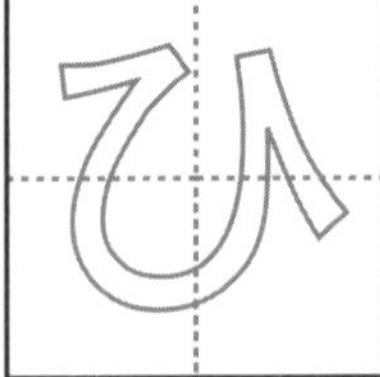

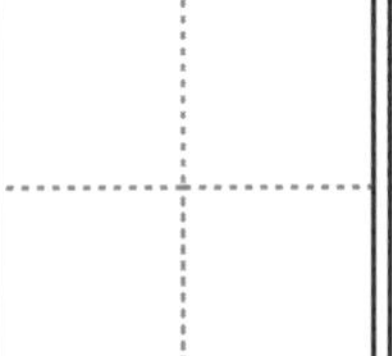

ヒーロー

***hii**roo*

superhero

Superheroes with such names as ウルトラマン (Urutoraman; Ultraman) and スペクトルマン (Supekutoruman; Spectreman) have long been the stars of Japanese television programs for young boys. Alas, most of these young hero-worshipers grow up to be what the Japanese call a サラリーマン (sarariiman; salaryman, or company employee) instead.

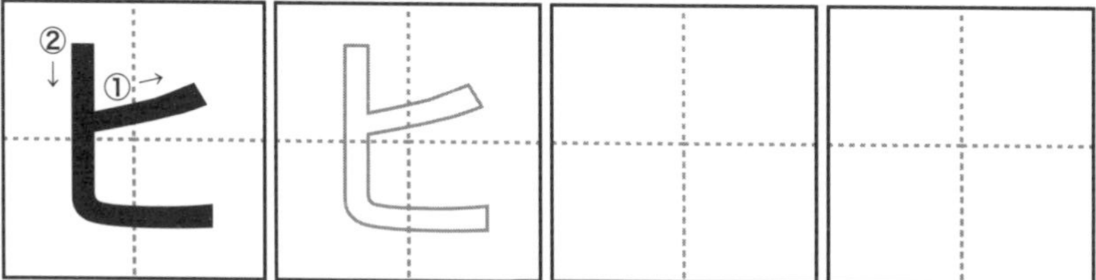

***fu**kutsu*

stomachache

Our friend here seems to be in a bit of pain. Must have been that bad すし (sushi) he had for lunch. Time to head to the local びょういん (byoin; hospital).

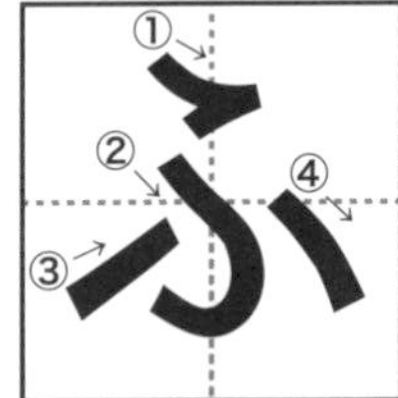

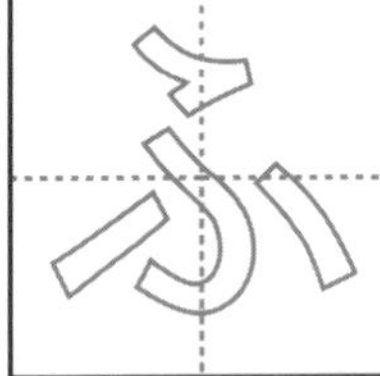

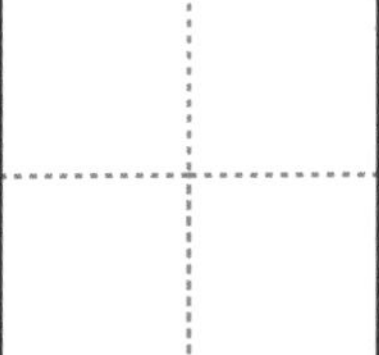

フクロウ

***fu*kuro**

owl

Is it possible to learn the secrets of the universe from a wise old owl? Perhaps. But you will probably have to adjust your schedule, as this particular やちょう (yacho; nocturnal bird) only teaches night classes.

 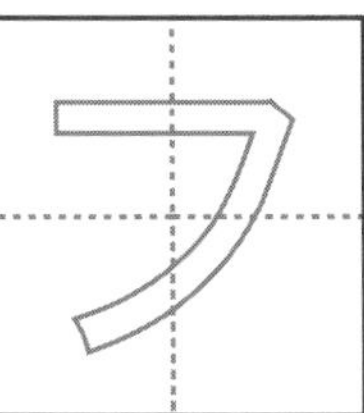 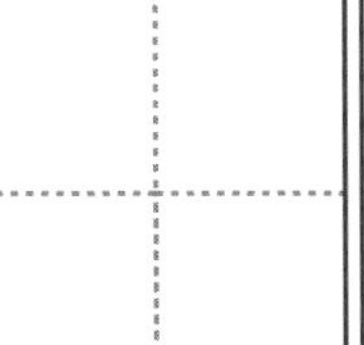 

へいあんじだい

***he**ianjidai*

The Heian Period

This period (794-1185) in Japanese history was marked by an unprecedented political stability that fostered the cultural refinement, or "Japanization," of the land. Buddhism began to flourish, and literary and artistic masterpieces were created. However, the period also saw the rise of the powerful samurai (さむらい) class of professional soldiers, whose fierce loyalty to regional warlords ultimately spelled the end for Heian tranquility.

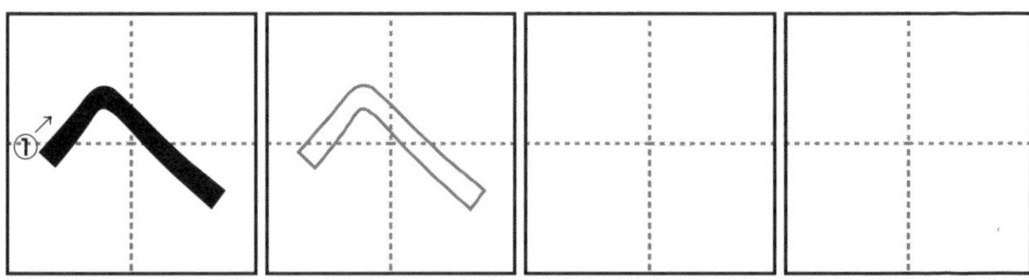

ヘルスメーター

***he*rusumeetaa**

health meter
(bathroom scale)

No matter how petite she really is, this young lady feels like a こぶた (kobuta; little pig). And the numbers don't lie. She's gained 2 ounces—that's right, 2 ounces!—since she last month.

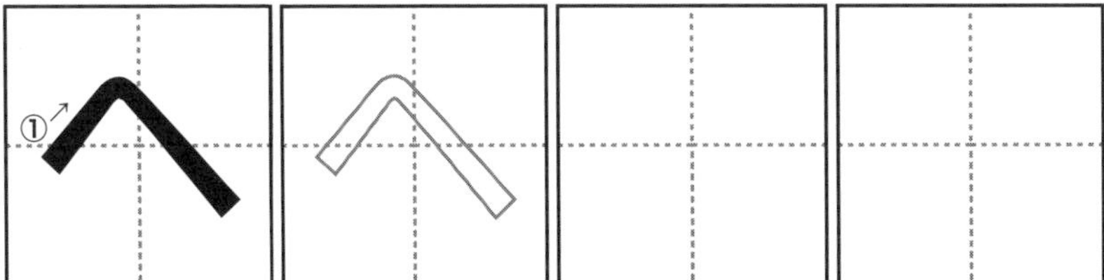

ほし

***ho*shi**

star

For the most part, people in Japan see the same "pictures" in the night skies as do North Americans and Europeans. But their names for many せいざ (seiza; constellations) are distinctly Japanese. For example, Lyra, the lyre, is called こと (koto), the name of a traditional Japanese stringed instrument. Just remember that when you wish upon a star, you can do so in any language.

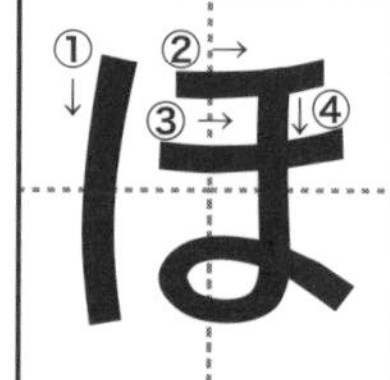

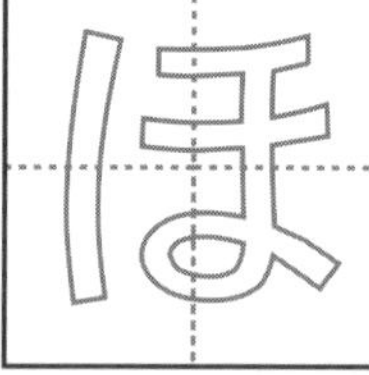

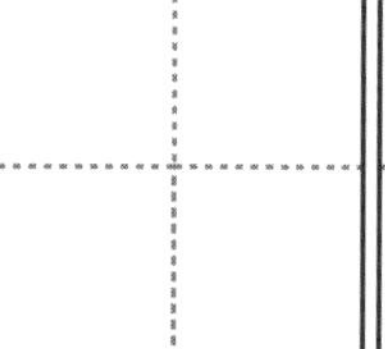

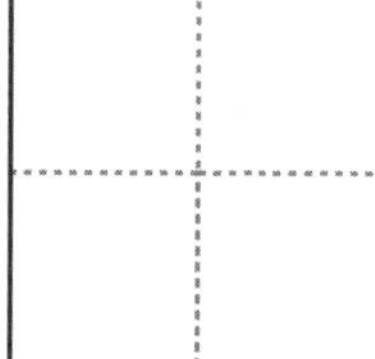

ホラーえいが

***ho**raaeiga*

horror movie

The first part of this word, ホラー (horaa), is how the Japanese pronounce the English word "horror." The second part, えいが (eiga), means "movie." The Japanese love horror movies, especially those about もののけ (mononoke; vengeful ghosts).

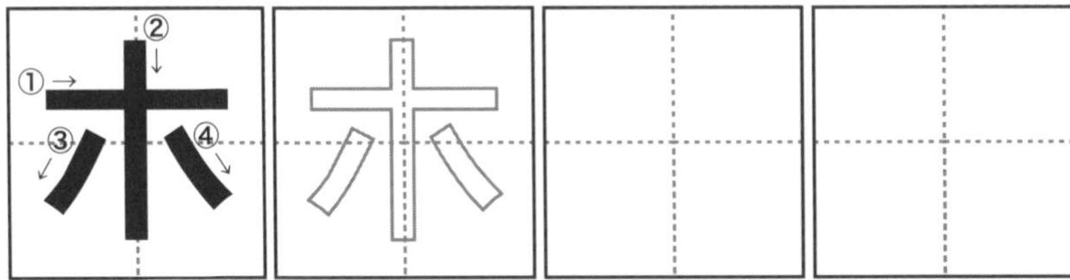

まり

***ma*ri**

ball

This is the traditional word for ball, although the katakana ボール (which, when pronounced, sounds like "ball") is quite common. The girl pictured here is dressed in a ゆかた (yukata; summer kimino) and ぞうり (zori, Japanese sandals).

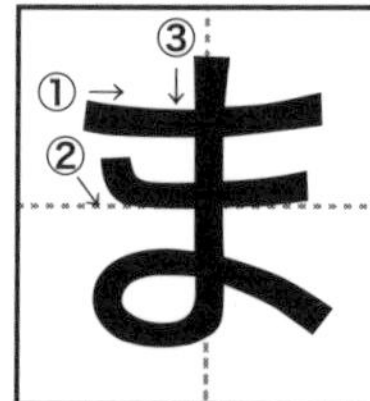

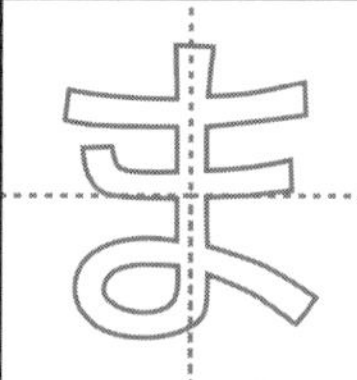

マフラー

mafuraa

muffler

Designer mufflers are very popular with じょがくせい (jogakusei; schoolgirls), and many boys also wear them. Favorite brands include バーバリー (Baabarii; Burberry) and エルメス (Erumesu; Hermes).

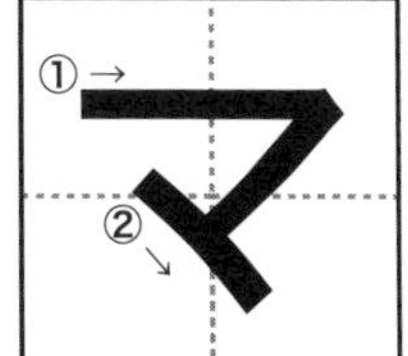

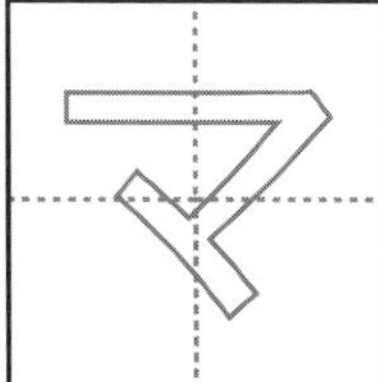

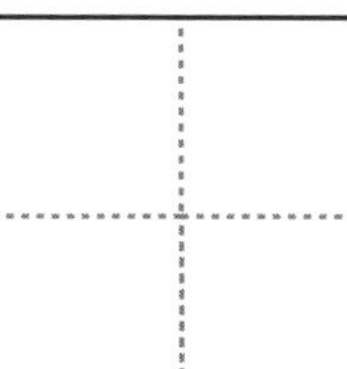

みこ

***mi*ko**

shrine maiden

In ancient times, miko were young women believed to be endowed with mystical powers that allowed them to divine messages from the かみ (kami; gods). Modern じんぐう (jingu; Shinto shrines) still employ miko, who today serve primarily as caretakers and assistants to the しんかん (shinkan; Shinto priests).

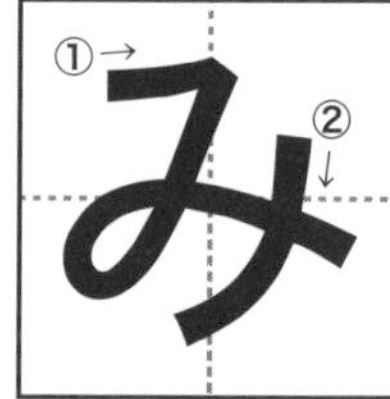

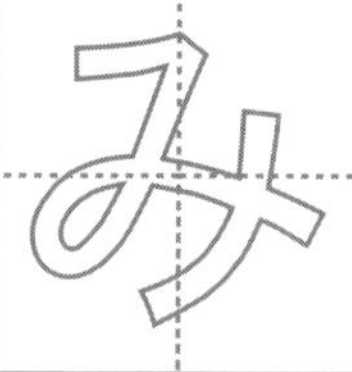

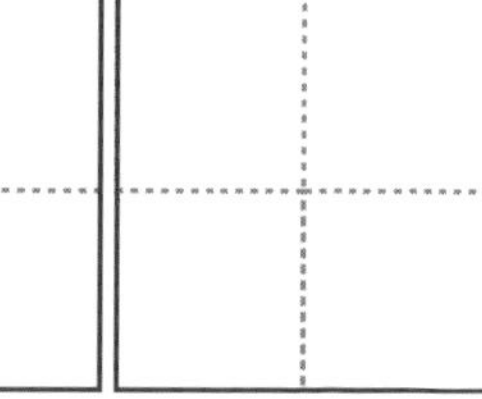

ミュージック

myuujikku

music

Japan has music for all tastes, ranging from easy-listening えんか (enka; love ballads) to J一ポップス (J-poppusu; Japanese pop) to ヴィジュアルロック (buijyuarurokku; literally, "visual rock," or hard rock). The traditional word for music is おんがく (ongaku).

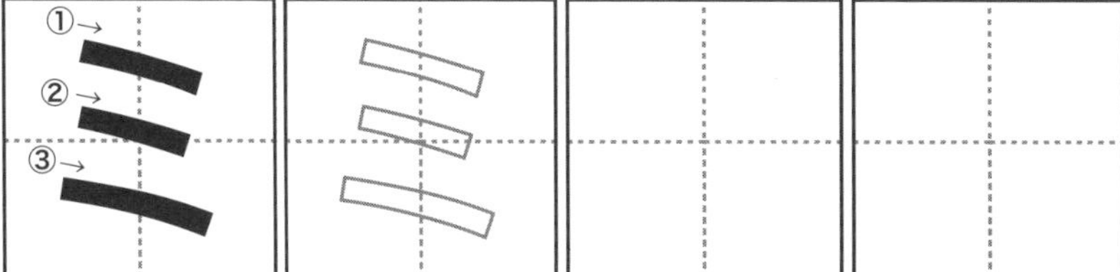

むきりょく

***mu**kiryoku*

lethargic

Hey, don't give up yet! If you've been studying them つぎつぎ (tsugitsugi; one by one), you've already learned more than half the kana in this book! がんばってください (Ganbatte kudasai; Keep going, you can do it)!

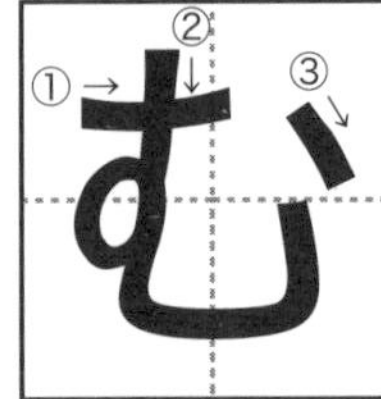

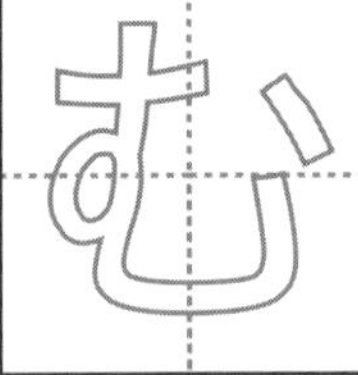

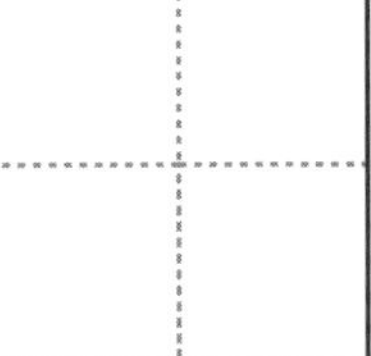

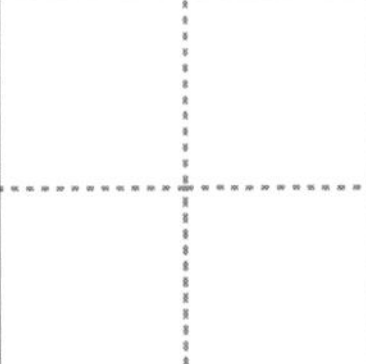

ムササビ

***mu**sasabi*

flying squirrel

With a wingspan of about 18 inches, the Japanese giant flying squirrel is among the largest of its kind in the world. The musasabi is a nocturnal animal and glides from one き (ki; tree) to another at a slow, graceful pace.

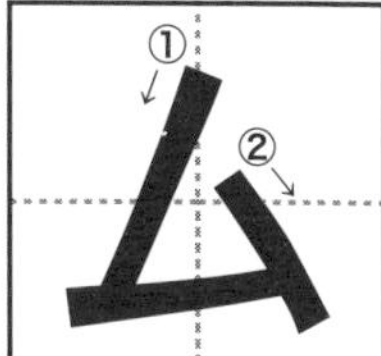

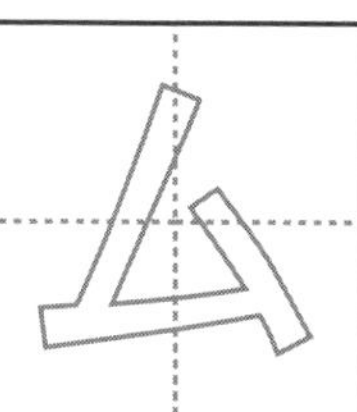

めざましどけい

mezamashidokei

alarm clock

The first part of this word, めざまし, comes from the verb めざめる (mezameru), which means "to wake." The ending, どけい, is an alternate way of pronouncing とけい (tokei), the generic word for "clock." We'll leave it to you to figure out what the word スヌーズボタン (sunuuzu botan) means.

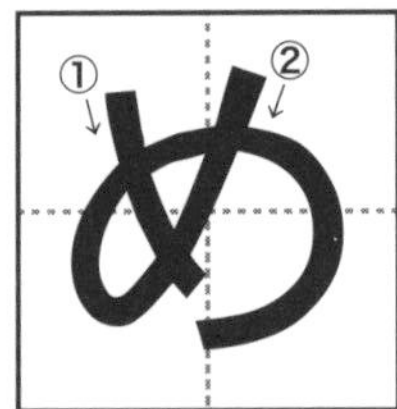

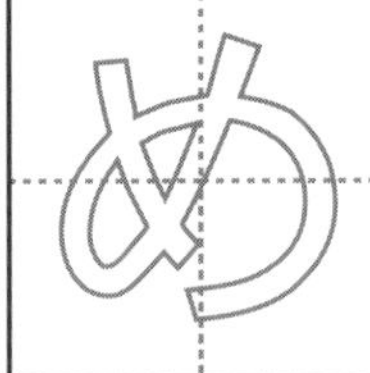

メガホン

***me*gahon**

megaphone

Students in Japan really know how to show their とうし (toshi; fighting spirit). At sporting events, they sing school songs, bang drums, blow horns and wave flags the entire time. Naturally, megaphones are an indispensable part of the cheering section's equipment.

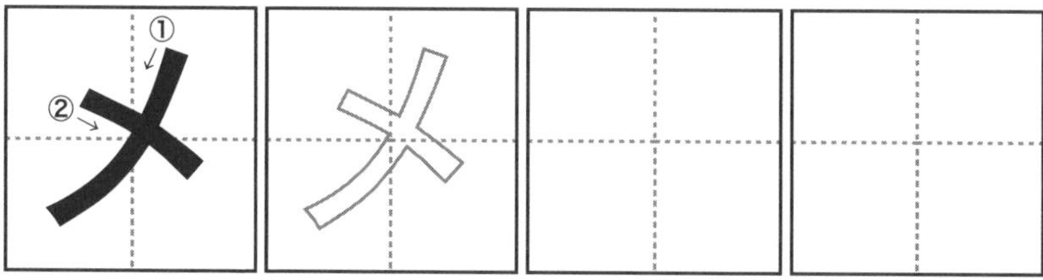

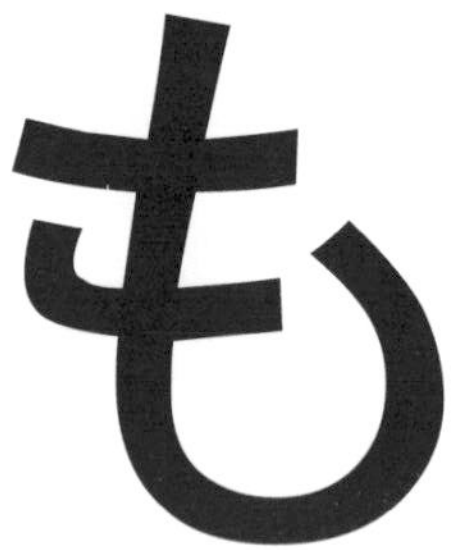

もぐら

***mo**gura*

mole

Because they like to dig late at night or early in the morning, moles often are the mascots of road crews in Japan. The sign behind these two rascals reads (in kanji), こうじちゅう (kojichu; under construction), and they are wearing Japanese-style hard hats.

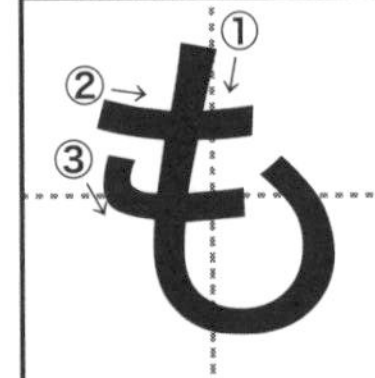

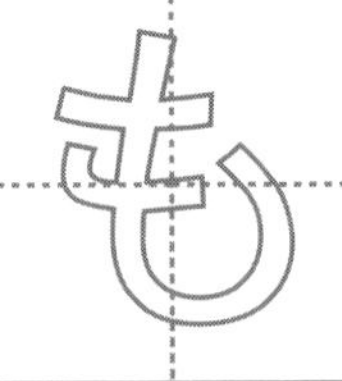

モップ

***mo*ppu**

mop

Man's best friend is also a boy's best buddy. The young owner of this shaggy いぬ (inu; dog) knows his pal could use a ヘアーカット(heaakatto; haircut), but he loves the mop top just the same.

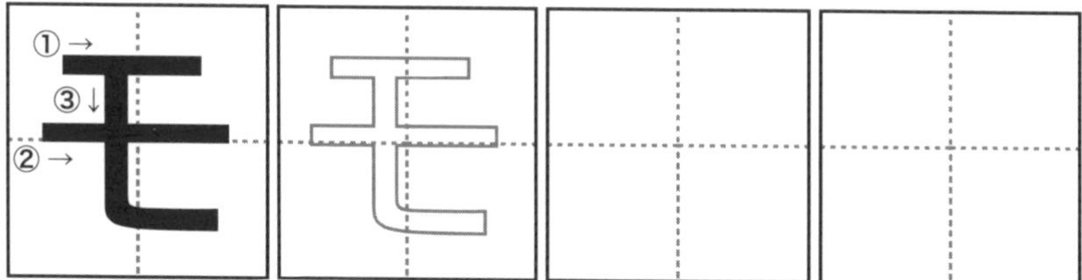

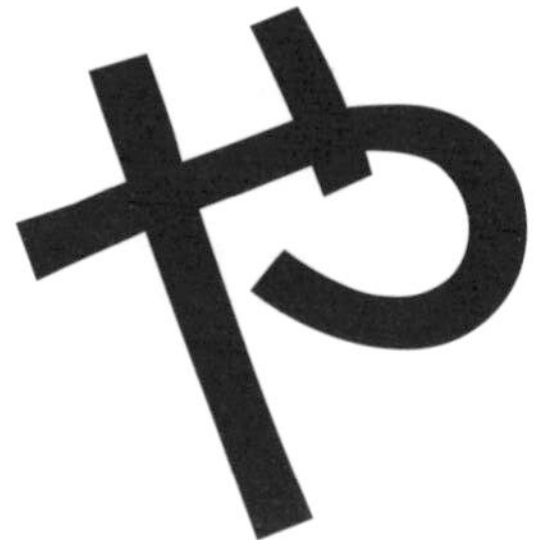

やじるし

***ya**jirushi*

direction arrow

Japanese ひょうしき (hyoshiki; road signs) are among the most confusing in the world, primarily because the streets in most cities crisscross one another in a way that defies logic. It's enough to make one's head spin.

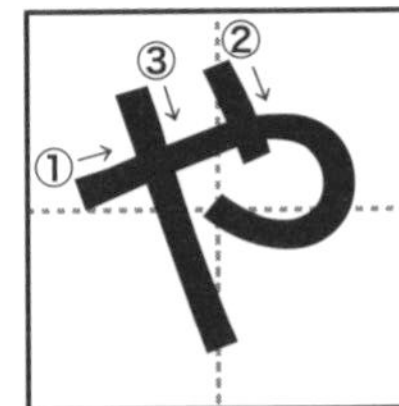

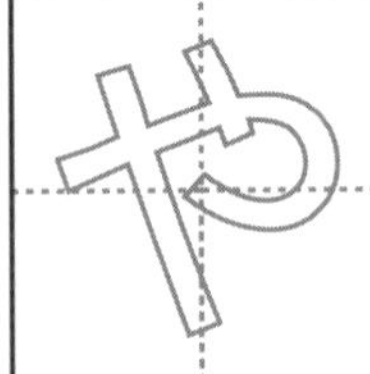

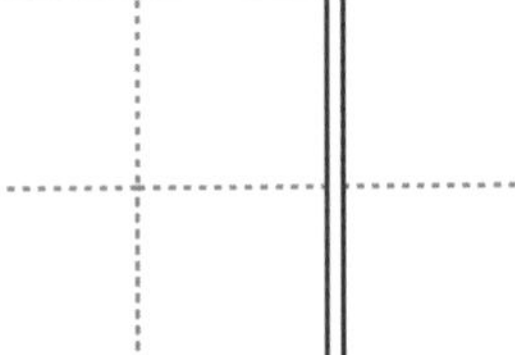

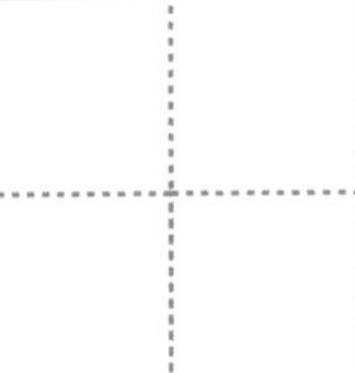

ヤカン

***ya**kan*

kettle

Here is a word that can be written in either katakana or hiragana. Literally, ヤカン (or やかん) means "medicine pot." Chicken スープ (supu; soup), anyone?

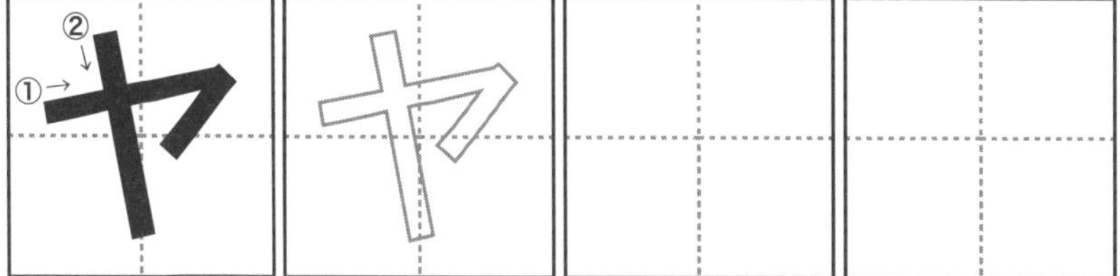

ゆきだるま

***yu*kidaruma**

snowman

The shape of a snowman somewhat resembles that of a Japanese だるま (daruma; dharma doll), hence the name ゆきだるま, with ゆき (yuki) being the word for snow. Dharma dolls are given as good luck charms to students, politicians, businesspeople and others who are trying to achieve difficult goals.

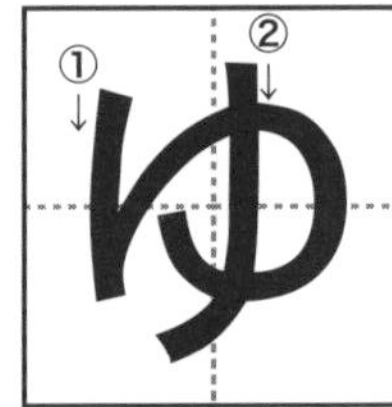

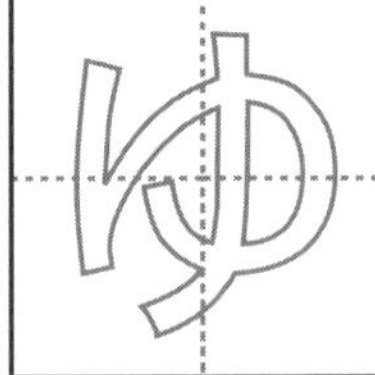

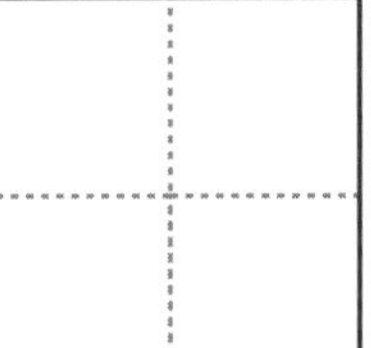

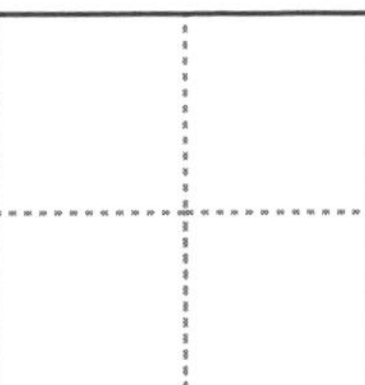

ユーフォ

***yu**ufuo*

UFO

UFO sightings are common in Japan, though most of them take place not in the sky but inside supermarkets. That's where conspiracy theorists can find UFO-brand instant やきそば (yakisoba; stir-fried noodles), which is sold in a flying saucer-shaped dish. Alien not included.

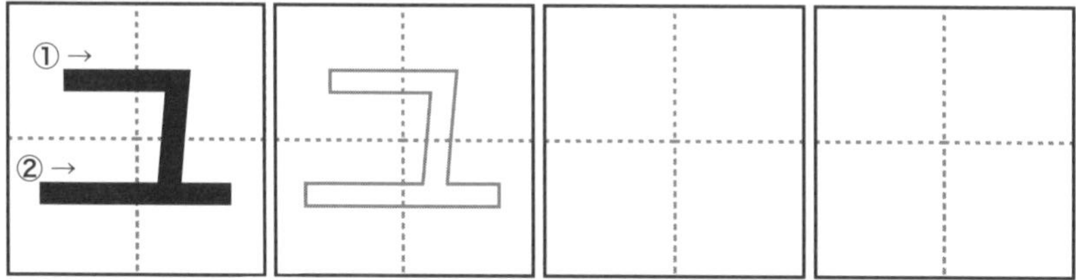

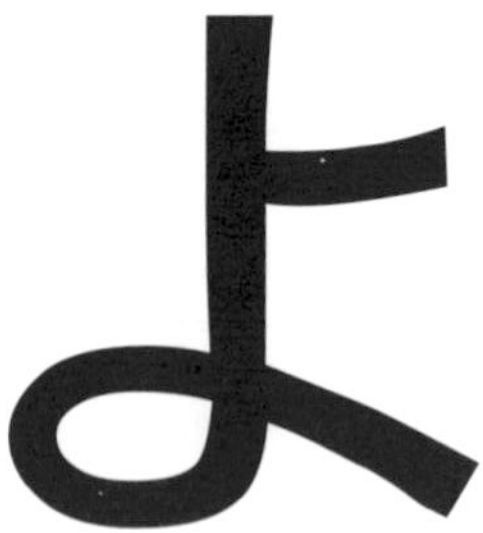

ようせい

***yo*sei**

fairy

Water sprites and other types of fairies hold a prominent place in Japanese みんぞくがく (minzokugaku; folklore). Especially beloved are the rascally water demons called かっぱ (kappa). These creatures are said to love cucumbers, which is why cucumber-filled sushi rolls are called かっぱまき (kappamaki; kappa rolls).

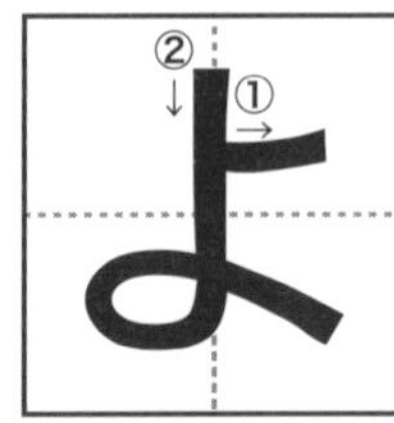

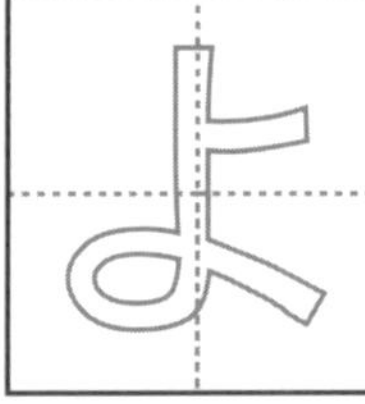

ヨーヨー

***yo**oyoo*

yo-yo

Children throughout the world have been playing with these simple toys for more than 2,500 years. The name itself comes from Tagalog, the native language of the Philippines, and means "come come" or "come back." In Japan, the numeral four is pronounced "yon" (よん), which sounds "yo," and thus the fourth day of the fourth month (April 4, or "yon-yon") is unofficially recognized by toy makers as Yo-Yo Day.

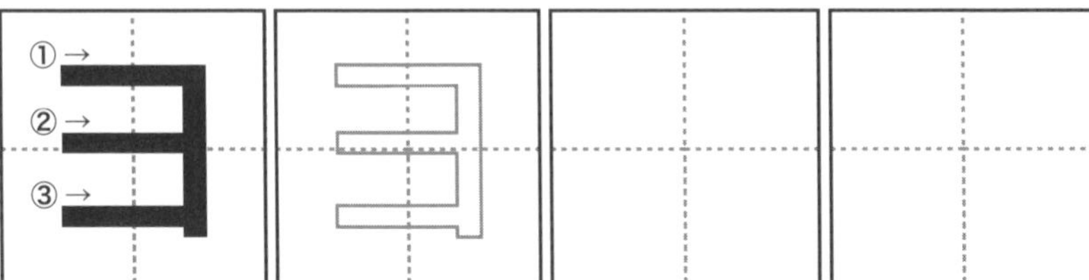

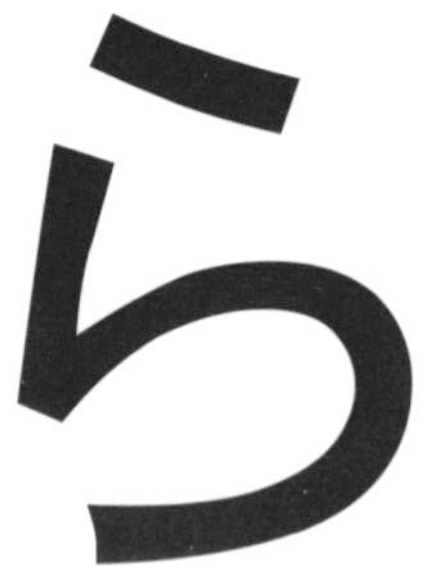

らいう

***ra*iu**

thunderstorm

The odds of being struck by らいこう (raiko; lightning) are 700,000 to 1. The odds that you've already memorized the first 72 kana in this ほん (hon; book) are 3 to 1. We like your chances.

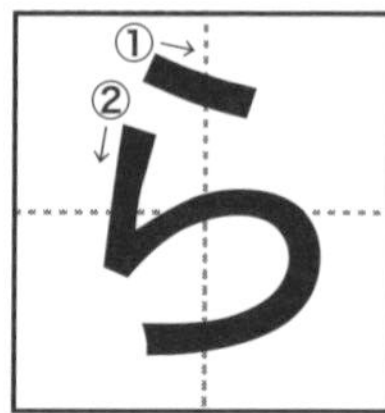

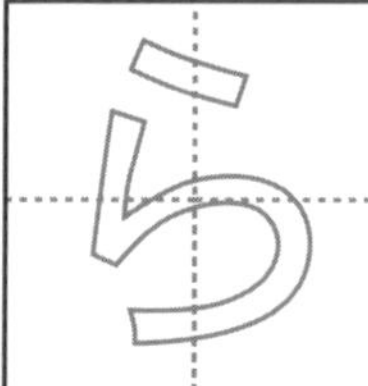

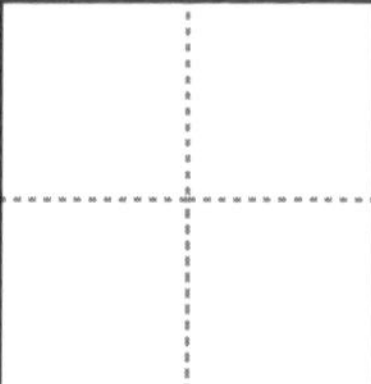

ライバル

***ra*ibaru**

rival

The expression "fight like cats and dogs" has a Japanese equivalent, but instead of a cat, the dog's rival is a monkey. The full expression is けんえんのなか (kenennonaka), which literally means "the relationship between a dog and monkey."

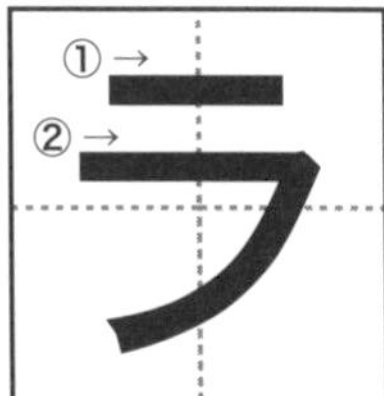

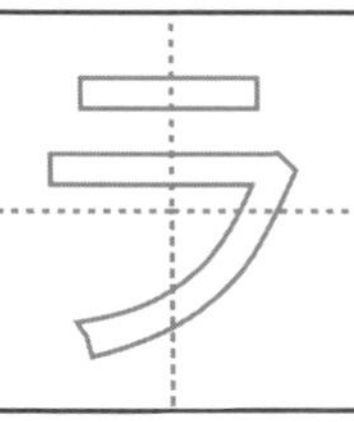

りゅう

***r*yu**

dragon

The dragons of Japanese legend closely resemble their Chinese counterparts, and are very fierce and powerful. Boys who are born during the たつどし (tatsudoshi; year of the dragon) are said to possess the characteristics that will make them leaders among men.

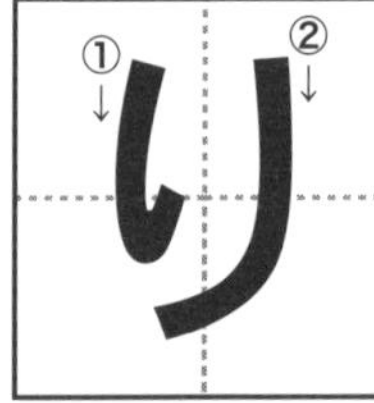

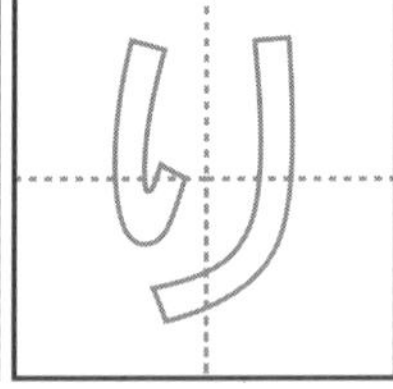

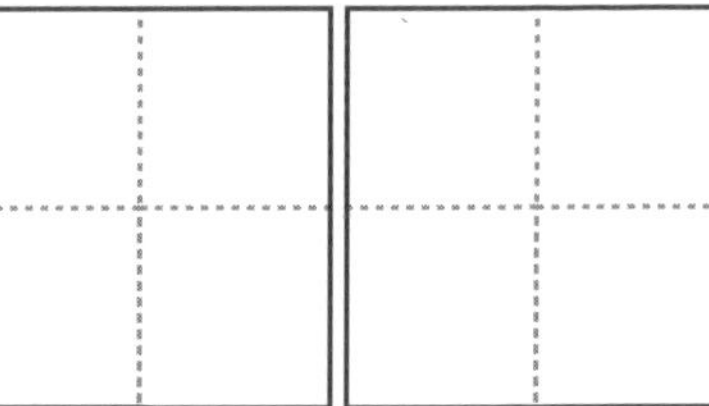

リサイクル

***ri**saikuru*

recycle

Tokyo's 28 million residents make it the most populous metropolitan area in the world. Remarkably, it is also one of the cleanest of all major cities, thanks in part to a comprehensive recycling program. In this picture, a young lady sorts garbage into three bins labeled プラスチック (purasuchikku; plastic), カン (kan; cans) and ビン (bin; bottles).

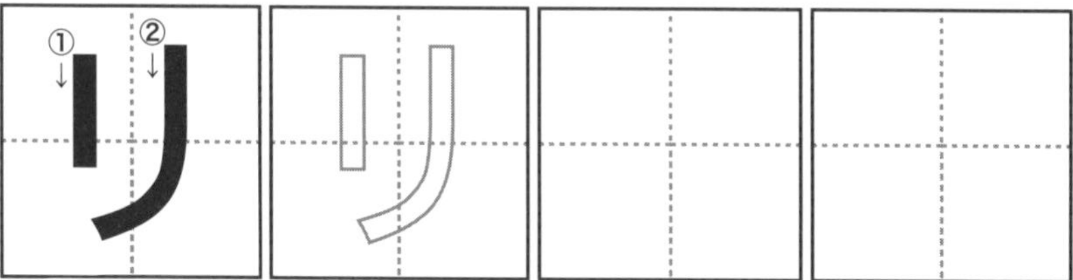

るいじ

***ru**iji*

similar

When you first started studying this book, you probably thought all hiragana and katakana looked the same. How about now? If you can tell the difference between characters such as る and ろ, and ク and ケ, you've just about mastered kana!

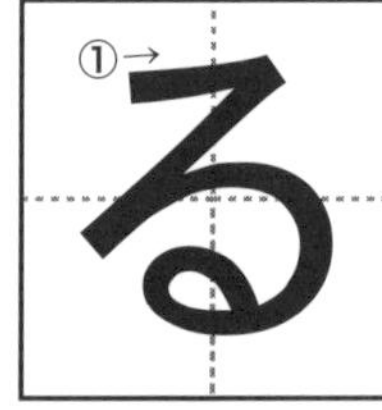

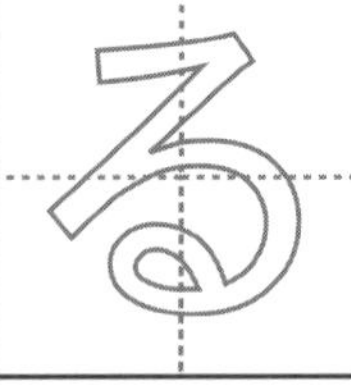

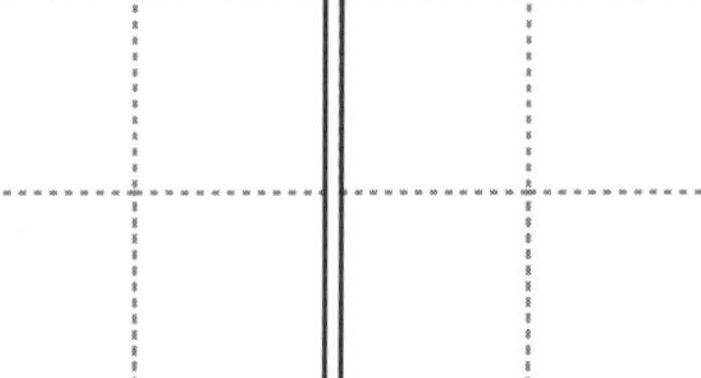

ルーペ

***ru**upe*

magnifying glass

There are several ways to say "magnifying glass" in Japanese, including むしめがね (mushimegane), which combines the words むし (mushi; insect) and めがね (megane; eyeglasses). The generic ルーペ derives from the German word "lupe."

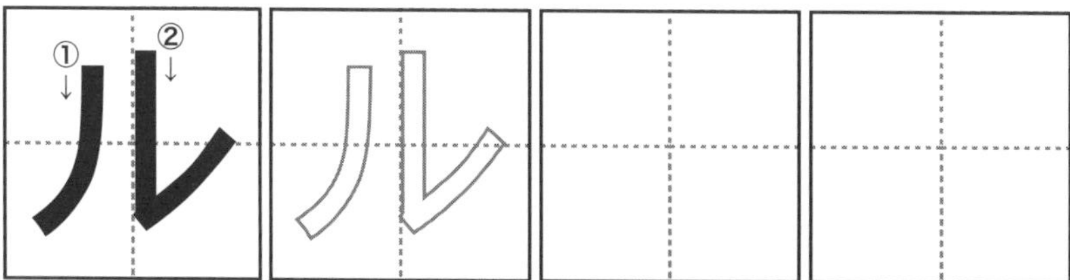

れいぞうこ

reizoko

refrigerator

Hungry for a late-night Japanese snack? Then climb out of bed and head to the refrigerator for some leftover なっとう (natto; sticky fermented soybeans), a few chunks of ばさし (basashi; raw horse meat), or maybe even a handful of deep-fried crickets. Oh, and don't forget the ぎゅうにゅう (gyunyu; milk).

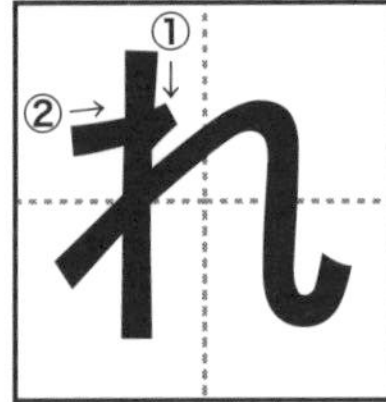

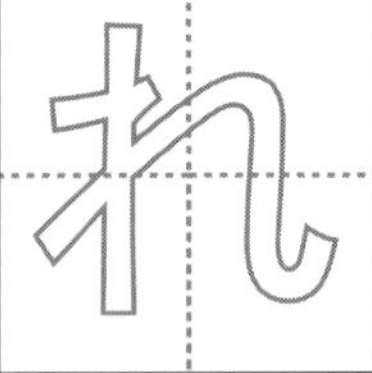

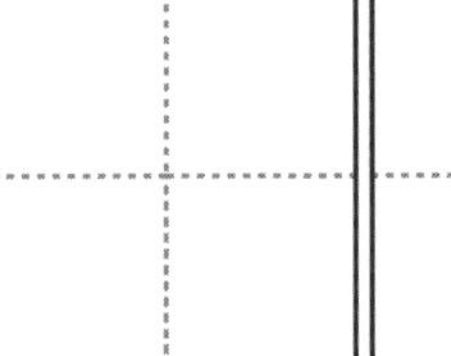

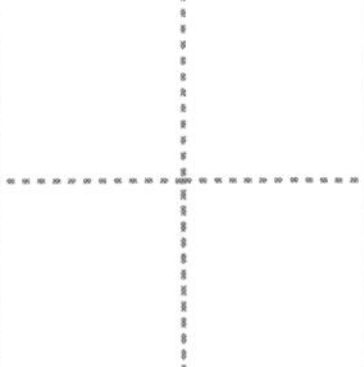

レインコート

reinkouto

raincoat

Planning to travel to Japan? Don't forget to pack a raincoat and かさ (kasa; umbrella). Tokyo alone gets an average of 60 inches of rain annually; other parts of the country are even wetter. Most of the downpours begin in early summer and culminate with the たいふう (taifu; typhoon) season in September.

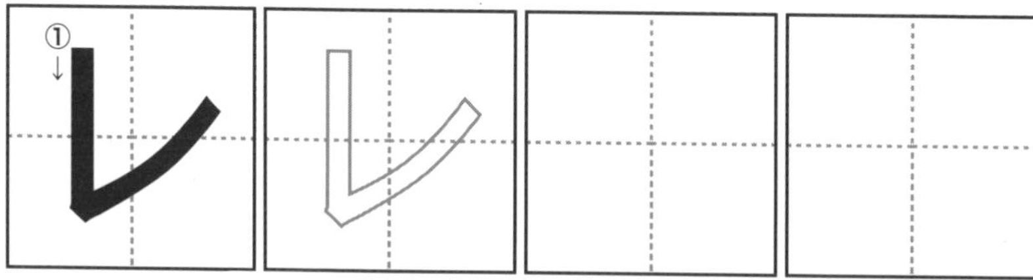

ろうそく

rosoku

candle

Nothing is more ロマンティック (romanchikku; romantic) than dining by candlelight with the one you love. The finest Japanese candles are made not from beeswax but rather wax from the はぜ (haze; Japanese wax tree).

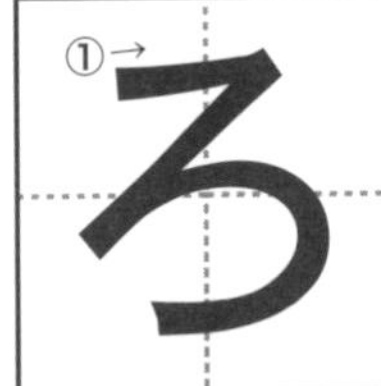

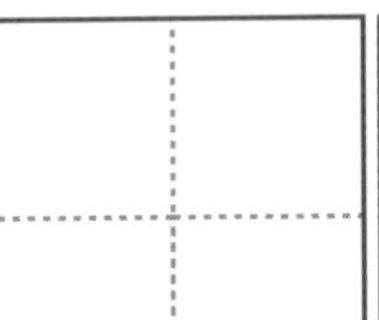

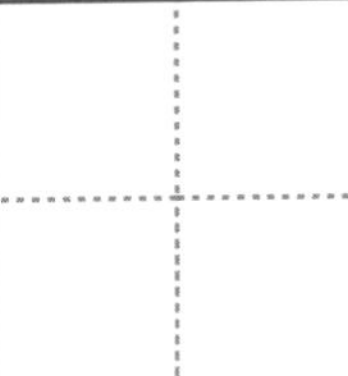

ロボット

***ro**botto*

robot

Japanese manufacturers have been making robot-type おもちゃ (omocha; toys) since the 1950s, when the first Robby the Robot windups were released. These sci-fi playthings have evolved over the years, and today Sony makes the highly sophisticated AIBO robotic dog. A brand-new AIBO costs about $2,000. An original Robby the Robot is now worth several times that amount.

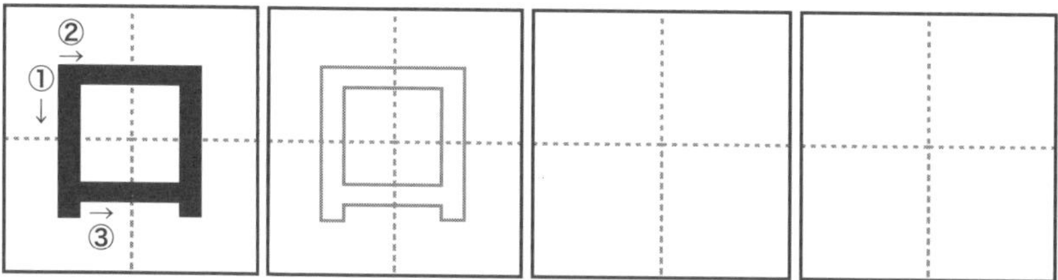

わらいごえ

***wa**raigoe*

laughter

Hey? What's so funny? Maybe someone just told him a わらいばなし (waraibanashi; humorous story). We hope he shares the じょうだん (jodan; joke) with us. The word for laughter combines わらい (warai; smile) with ごえ (goe; voice), and therefore can be interpreted as "smile with a voice."

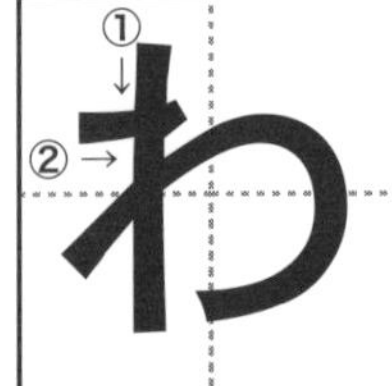

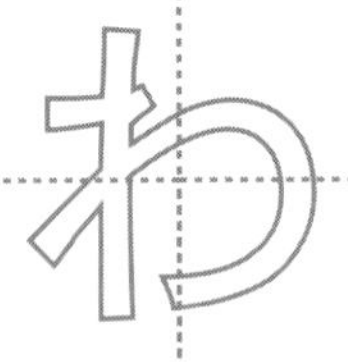

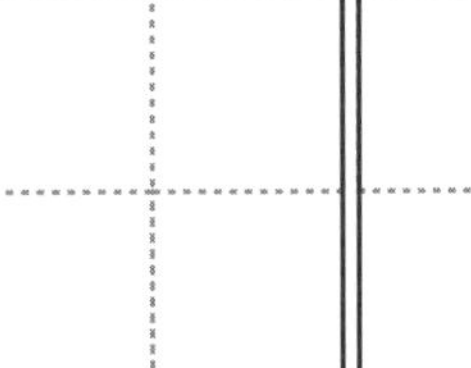

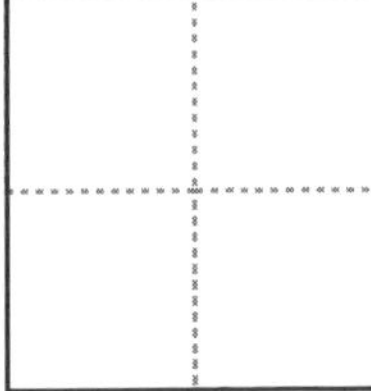

ワンピース

***wa**npiisu*

one-piece dress

The English word "one" is used often in Japanese. Some examples: ワンサイド (wansaido; one-sided), ワンマンショー (wanmansho; one-man show) and ワンステップずつ (wansuteppuzutsu; one step at a time).

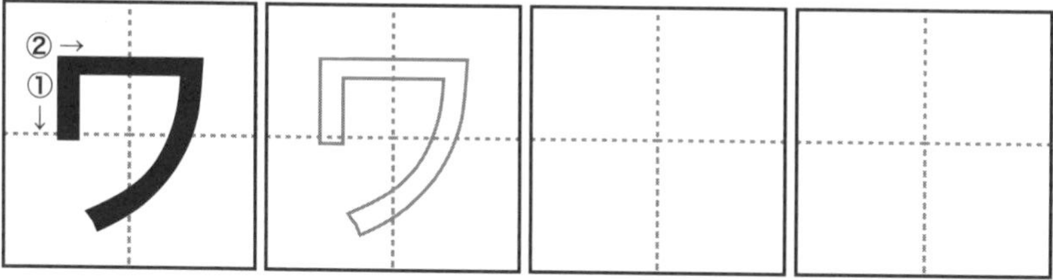

This character, romanized as "o" but pronounced either "o" or "wo," is used strictly as a particle, as in the phrase ほんをよむ (hon o yomu; read a book), where ほん (hon) means book, よむ (yomu) is the verb "to read" and を is the particle.

The ん character is pronounced as "n" or "m" and is the only consonant sound in which a Japanese word can end (for example, ほん, hon; book). This kana also can be used in the middle of a word, though never at the beginning.

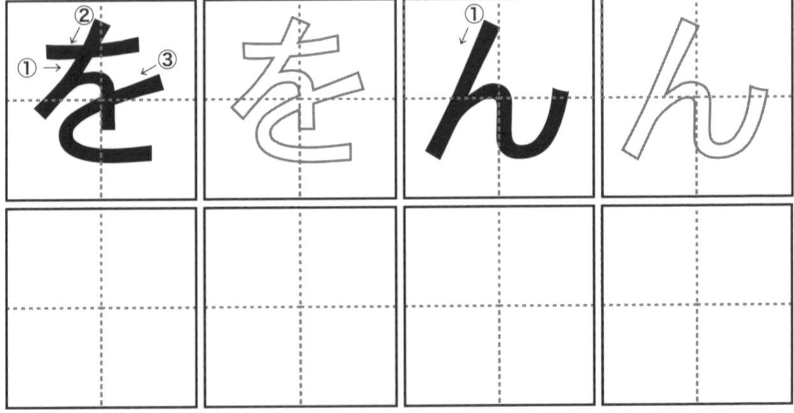

The katakana equivalent of the hiragana particle を is almost never used in formal Japanese writing. We present the kana here for reference only.

The same rules that govern the use of the hiragana ん also apply to ン in katakana. It is the only consonant sound to appear at the end of a word, and is never used at the beginning of one.

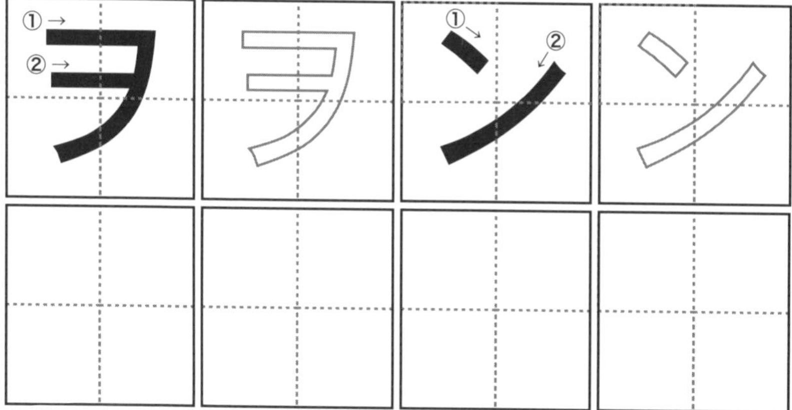

PRACTICE SECTION

ALSO AVAILABLE FROM

MANGA UNIVERSITY

ON SALE NOW

ISBN 4-921205-02-7

カタカナ (Katakana)

ア a	イ i	ウ u	エ e	オ o
カ ka	キ ki	ク ku	ケ ke	コ ko
サ sa	シ shi	ス su	セ se	ソ so
タ ta	チ chi	ツ tsu	テ te	ト to
ナ na	ニ ni	ヌ nu	ネ ne	ノ no
ハ ha	ヒ hi	フ fu	ヘ he	ホ ho
マ ma	ミ mi	ム mu	メ me	モ mo
ヤ ya		ユ yu		ヨ yo
ラ ra	リ ri	ル ru	レ re	ロ ro
ワ wa				ヲ wo
				ン n

ガ ga	ギ gi	グ gu	ゲ ge	ゴ go
ザ za	ジ ji	ズ zu	ゼ ze	ゾ zo
ダ da	ヂ ji	ヅ zu	デ de	ド do
バ ba	ビ bi	ブ bu	ベ be	ボ bo
パ pa	ピ pi	プ pu	ペ pe	ポ po